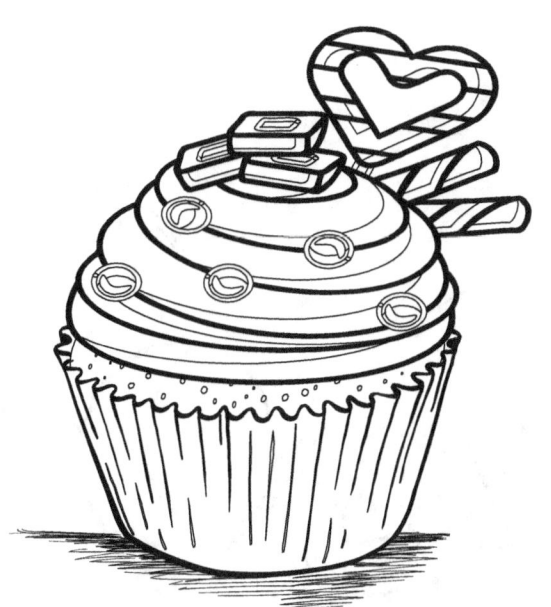

thank you for purchase

have fun with colouring pages full of super cute cupcakes.
For children of all ages, teenagers and even adults, enjoy and relax.
To ensure you have the best experience using this colouring book and to prevent bleeding, although the illustrations are on one side, we recommend colouring with pencils.

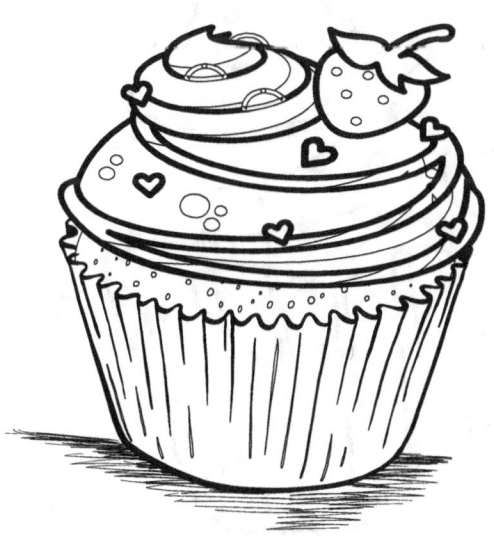
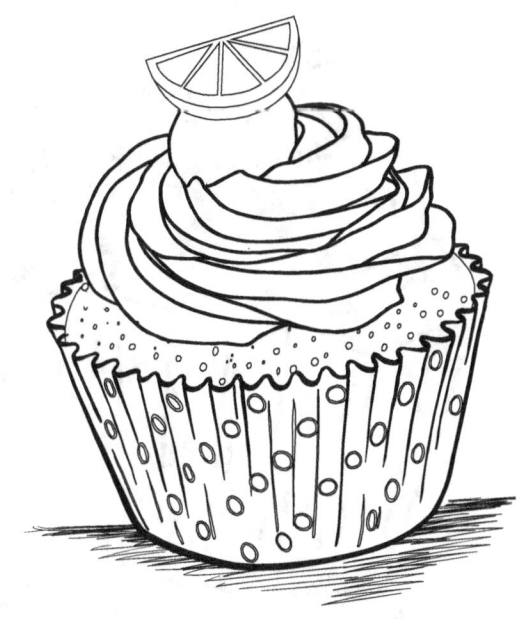

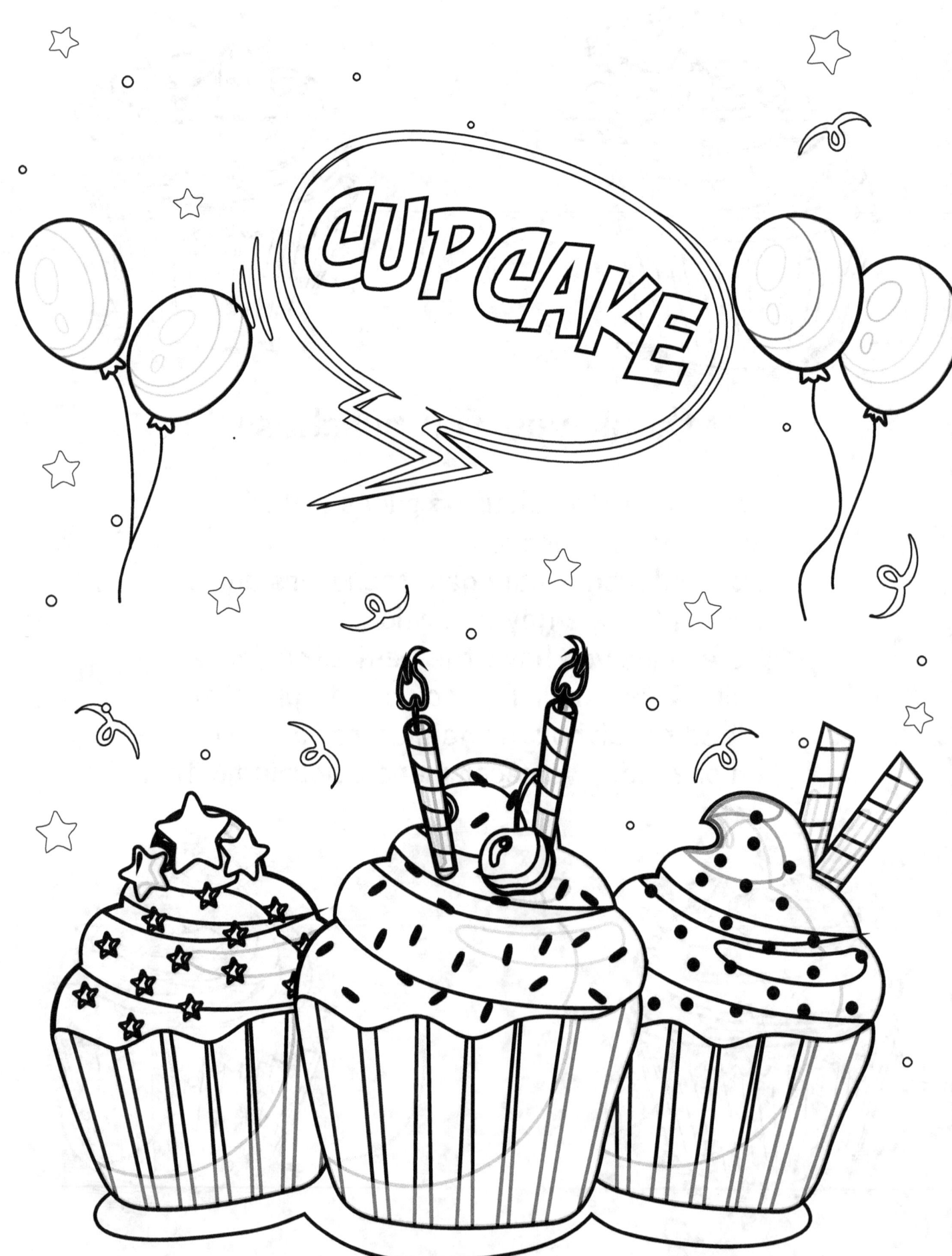

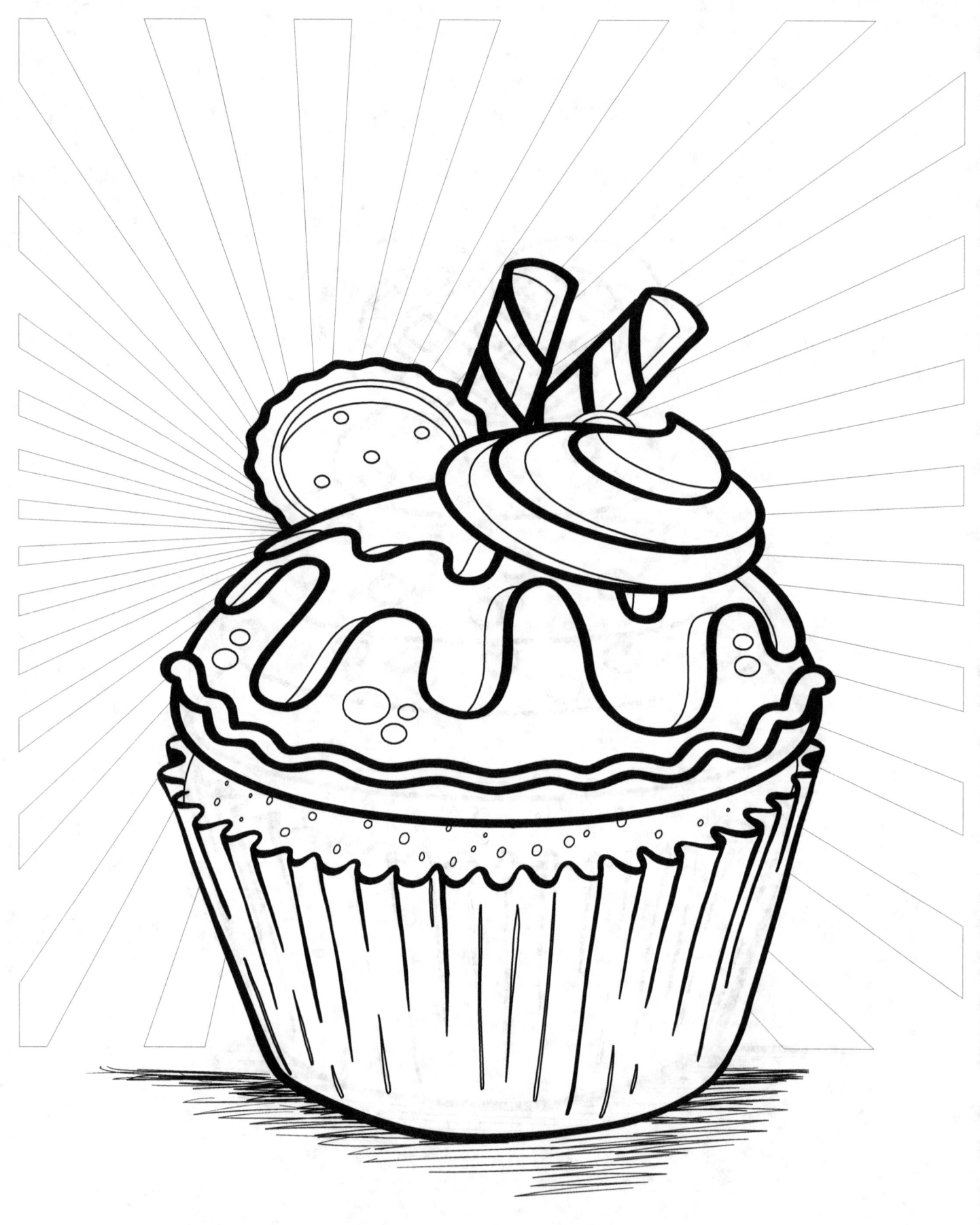

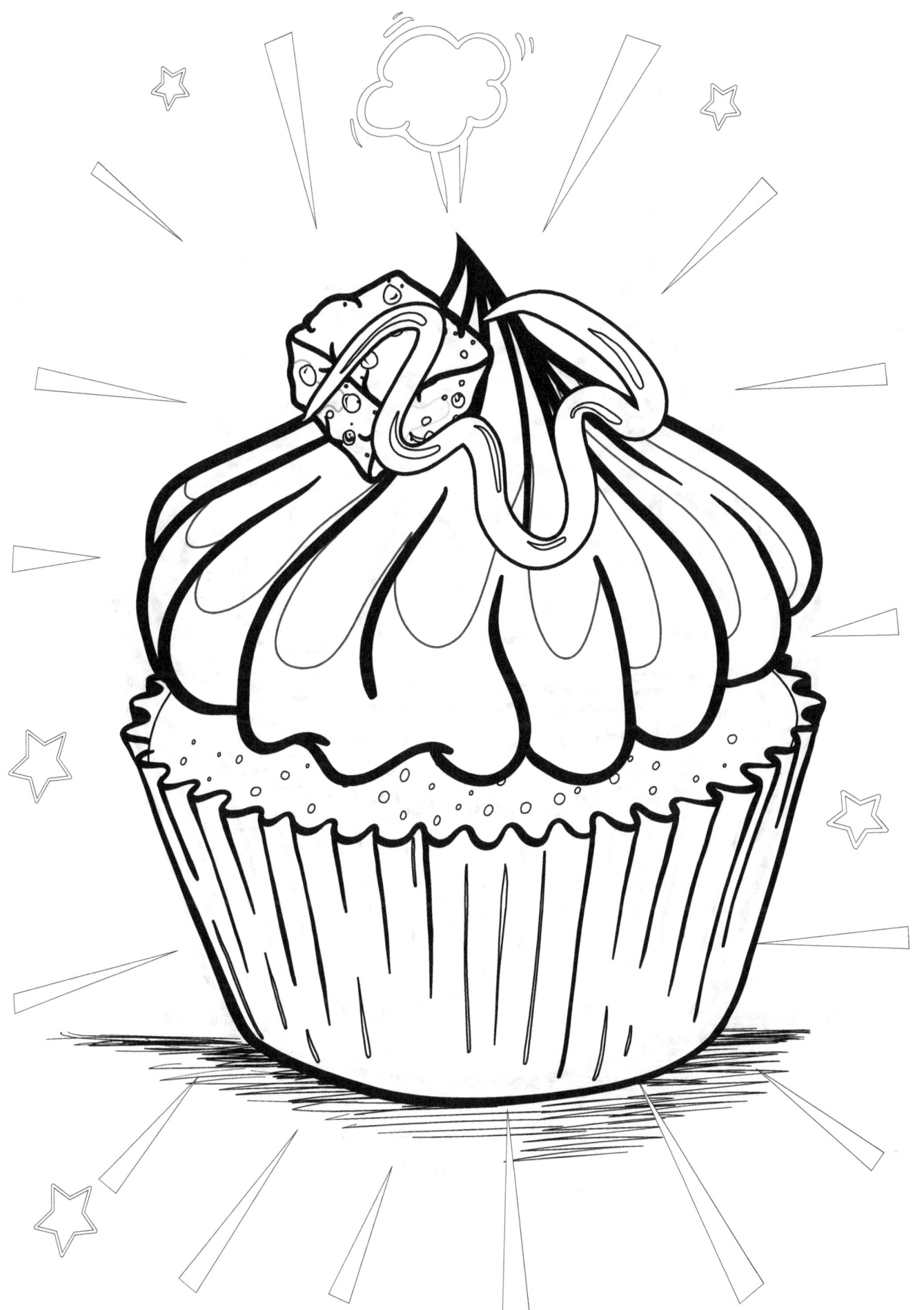

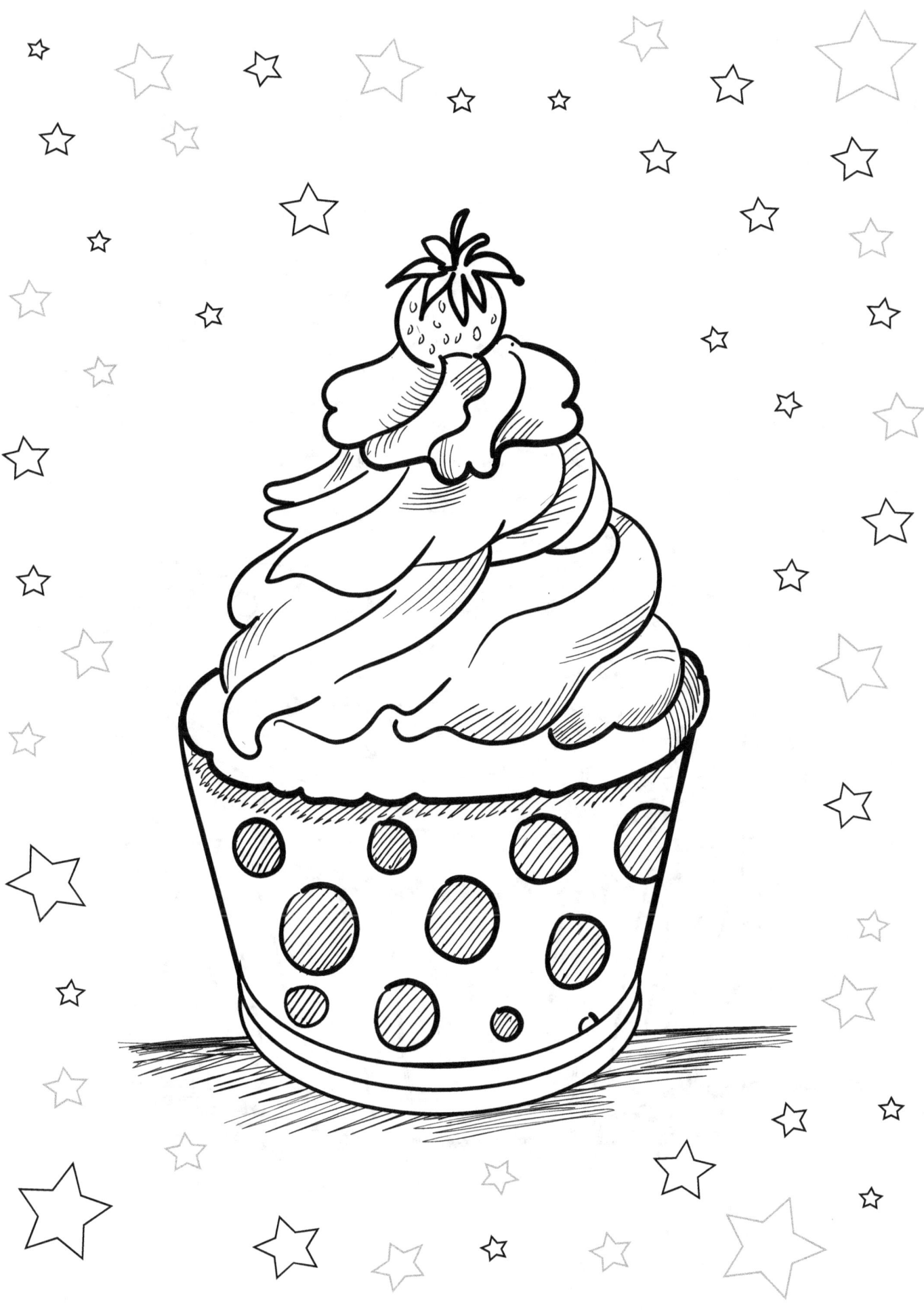

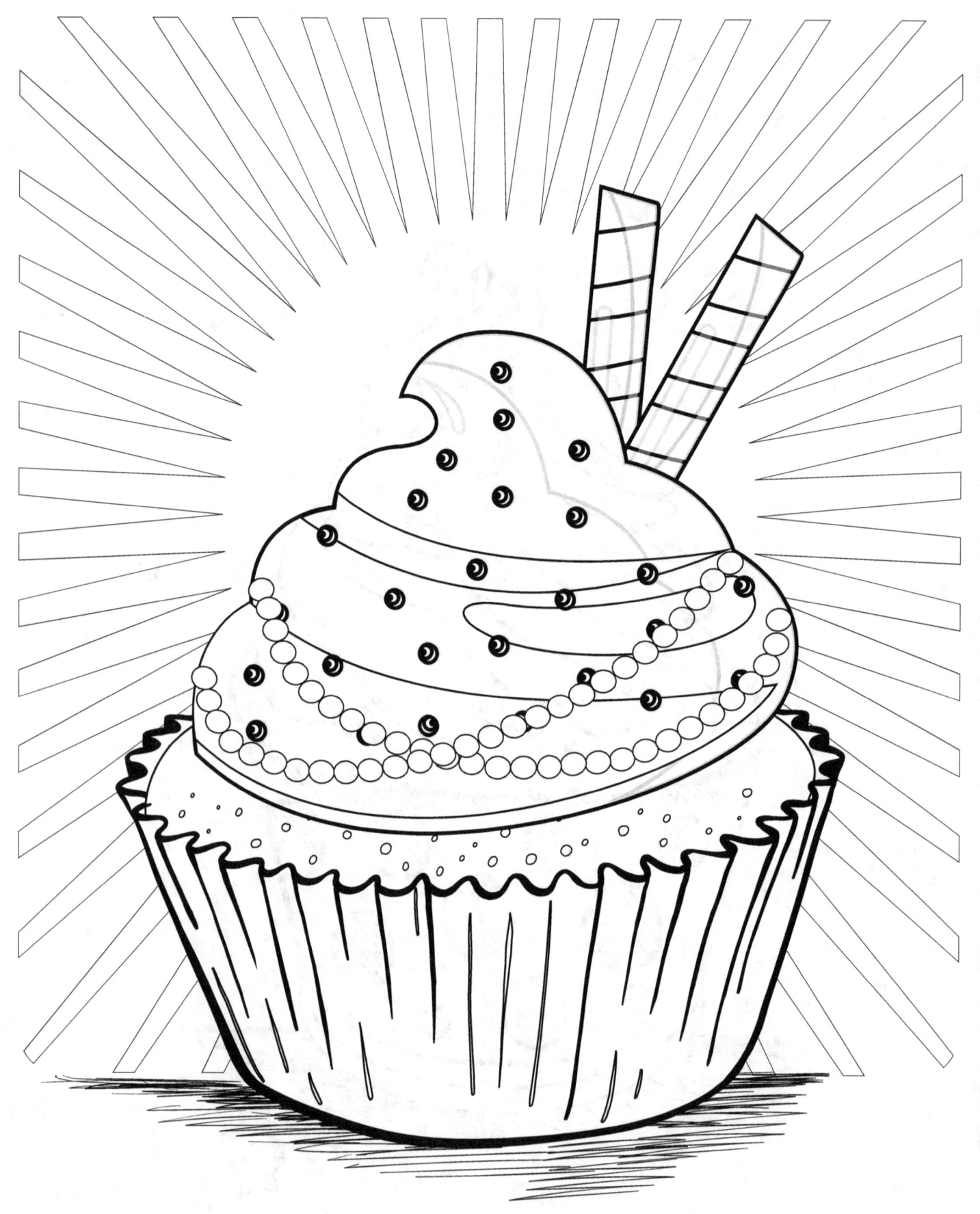

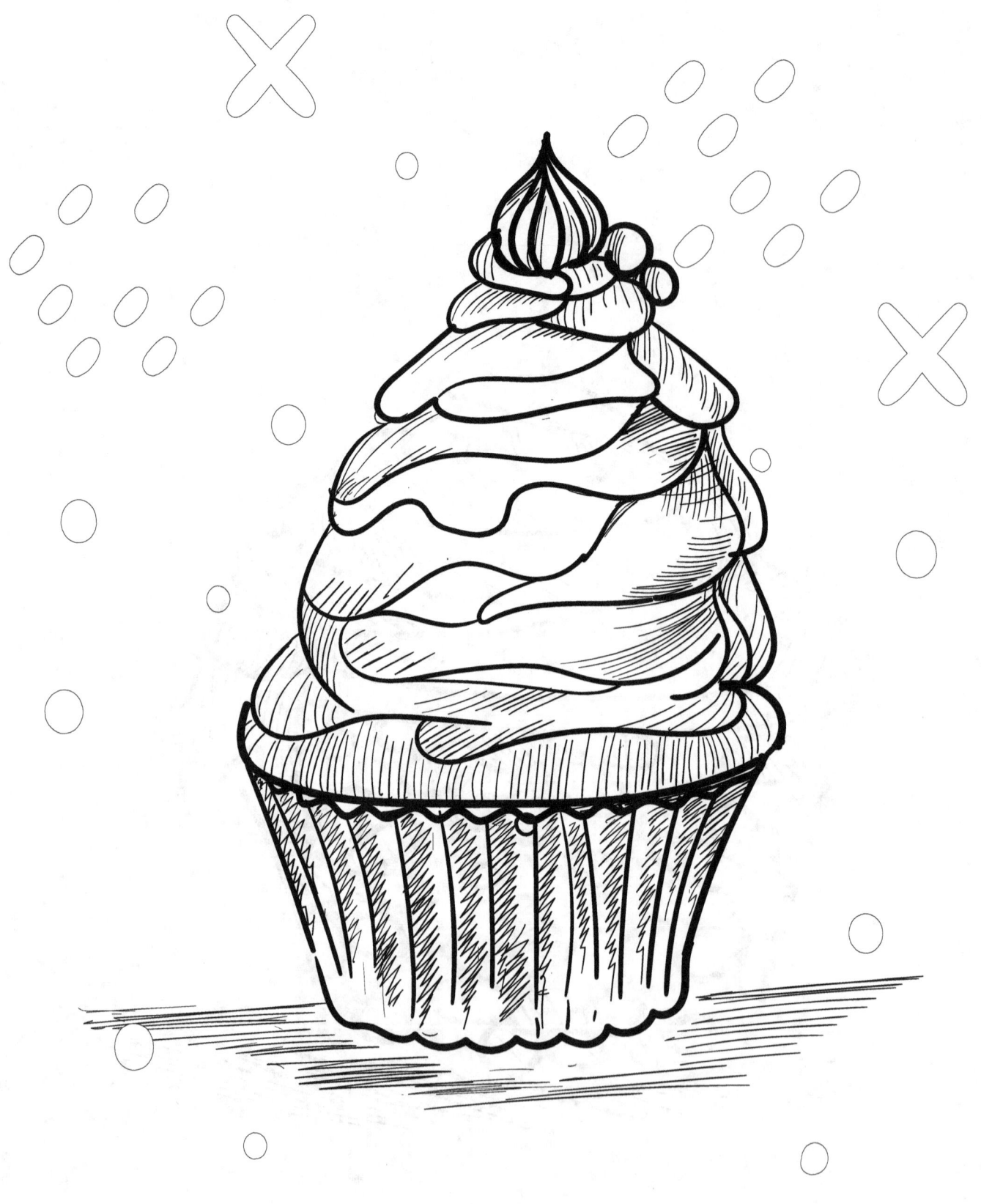

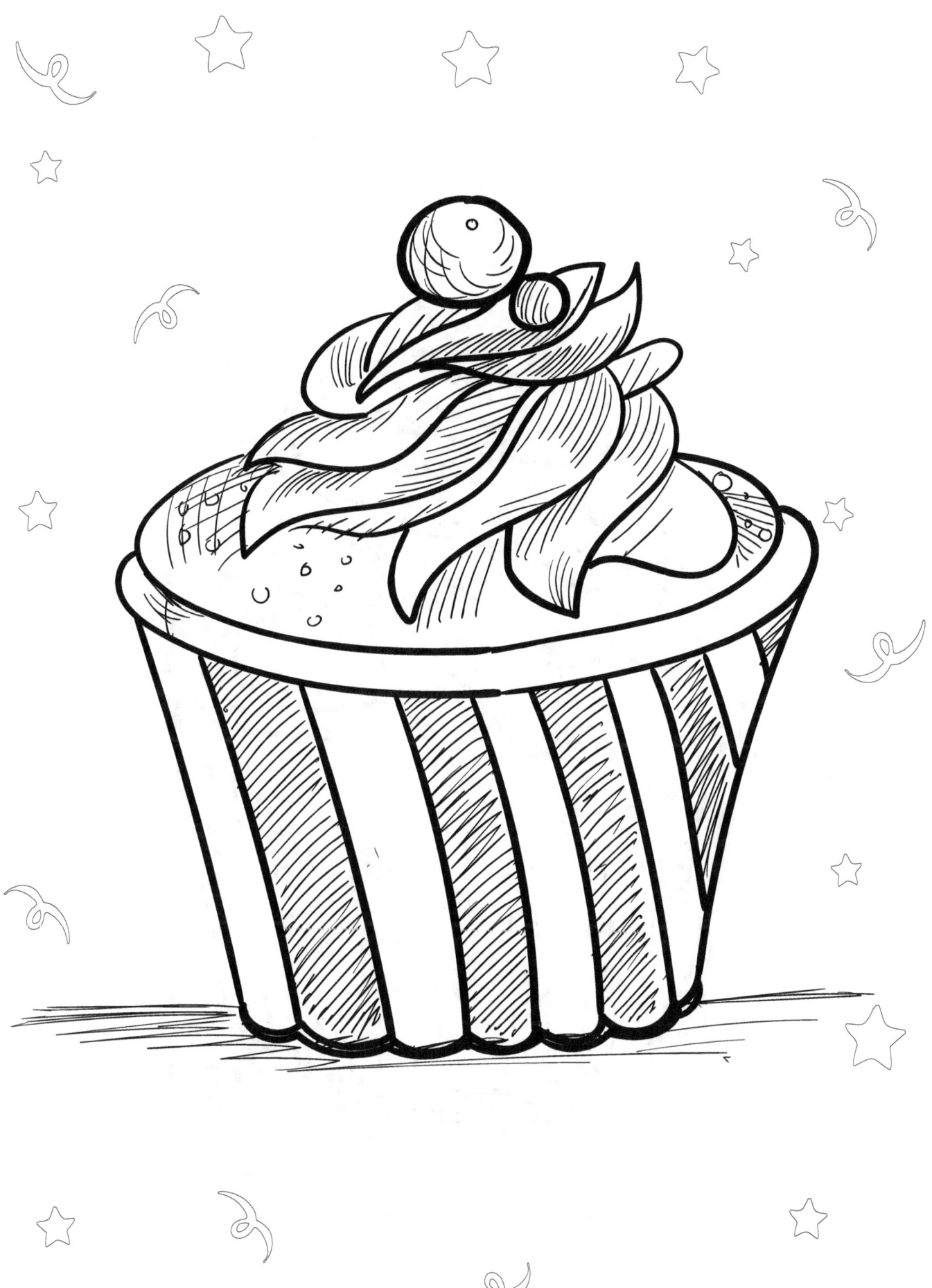

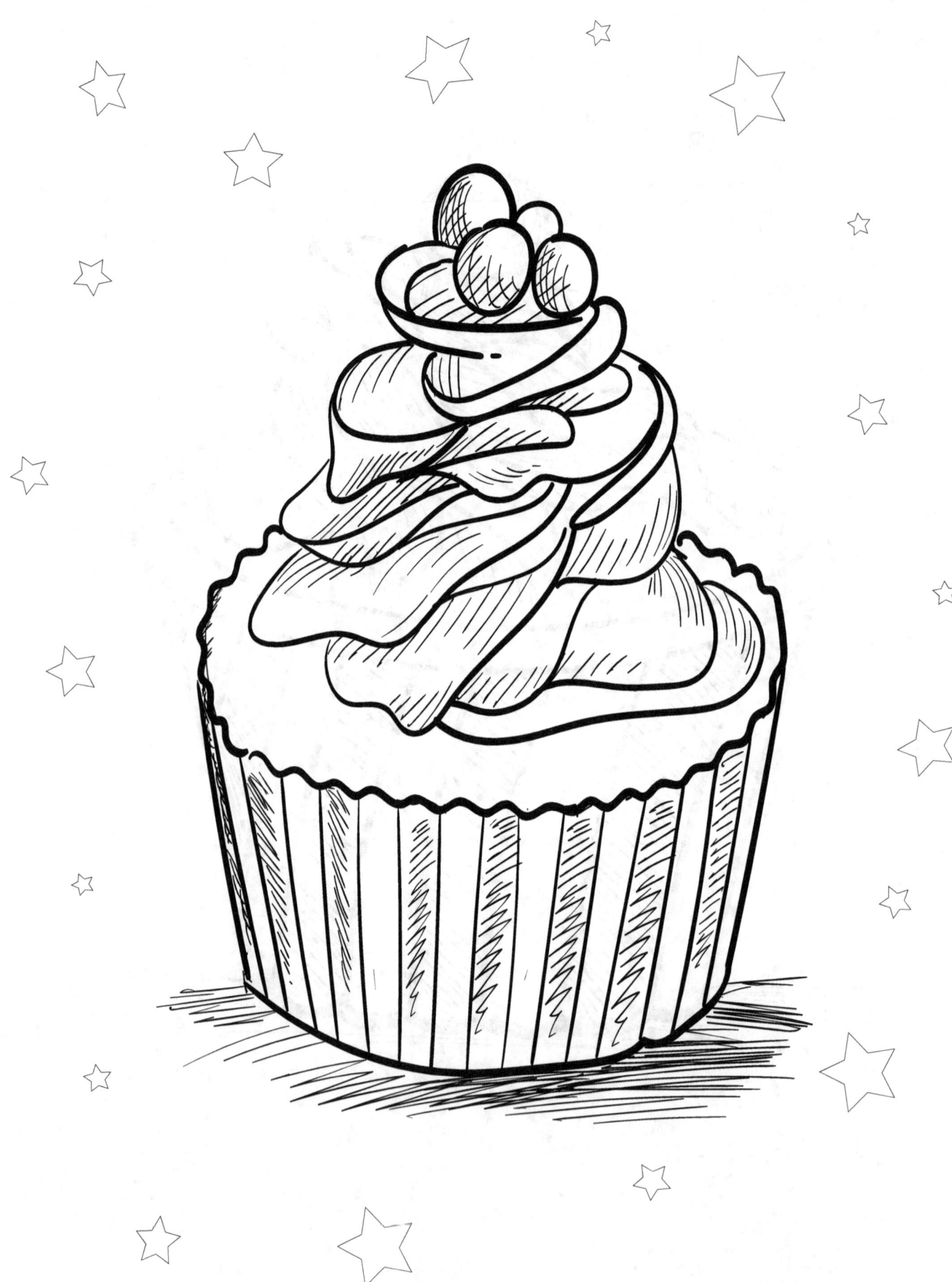

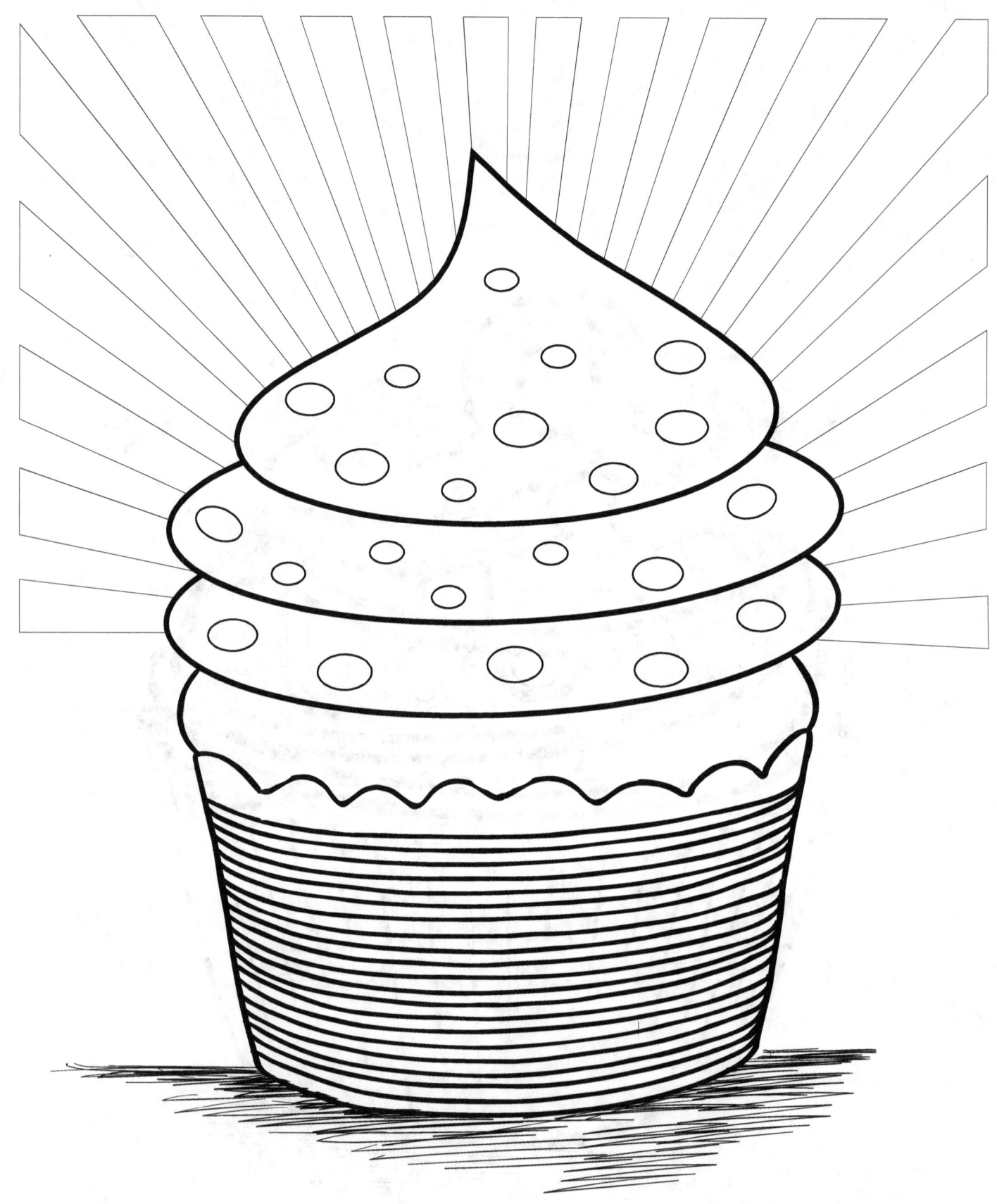

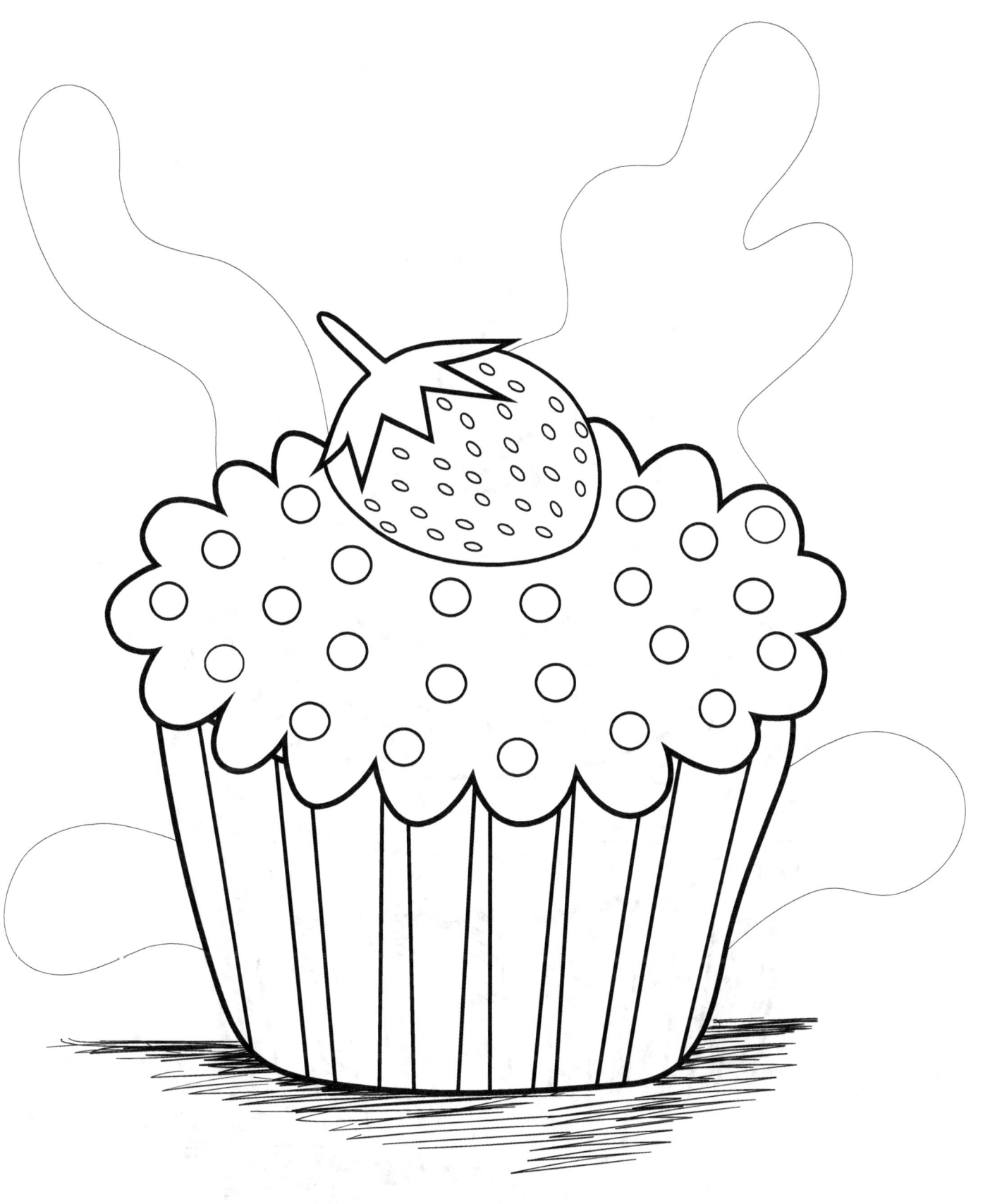

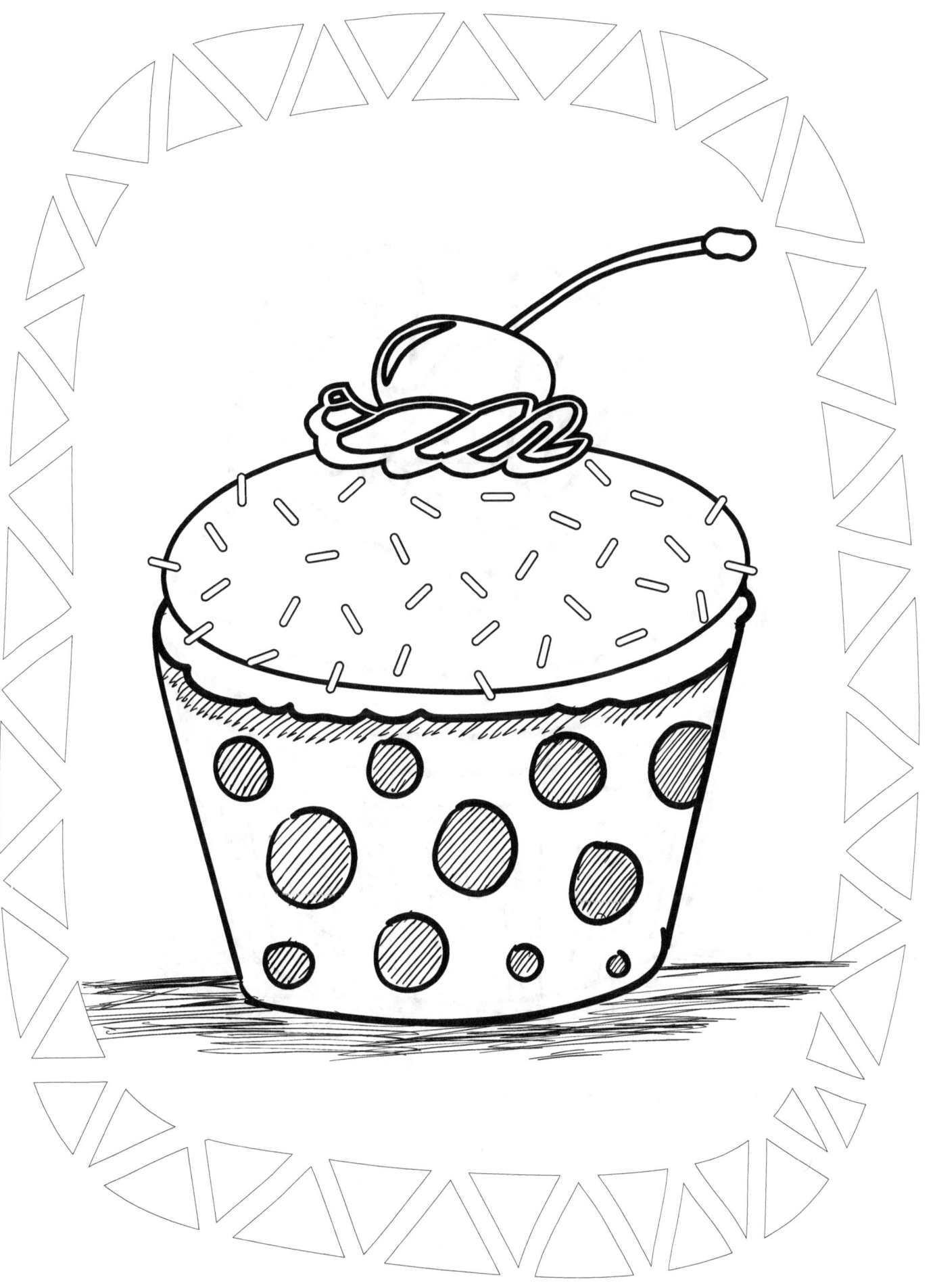

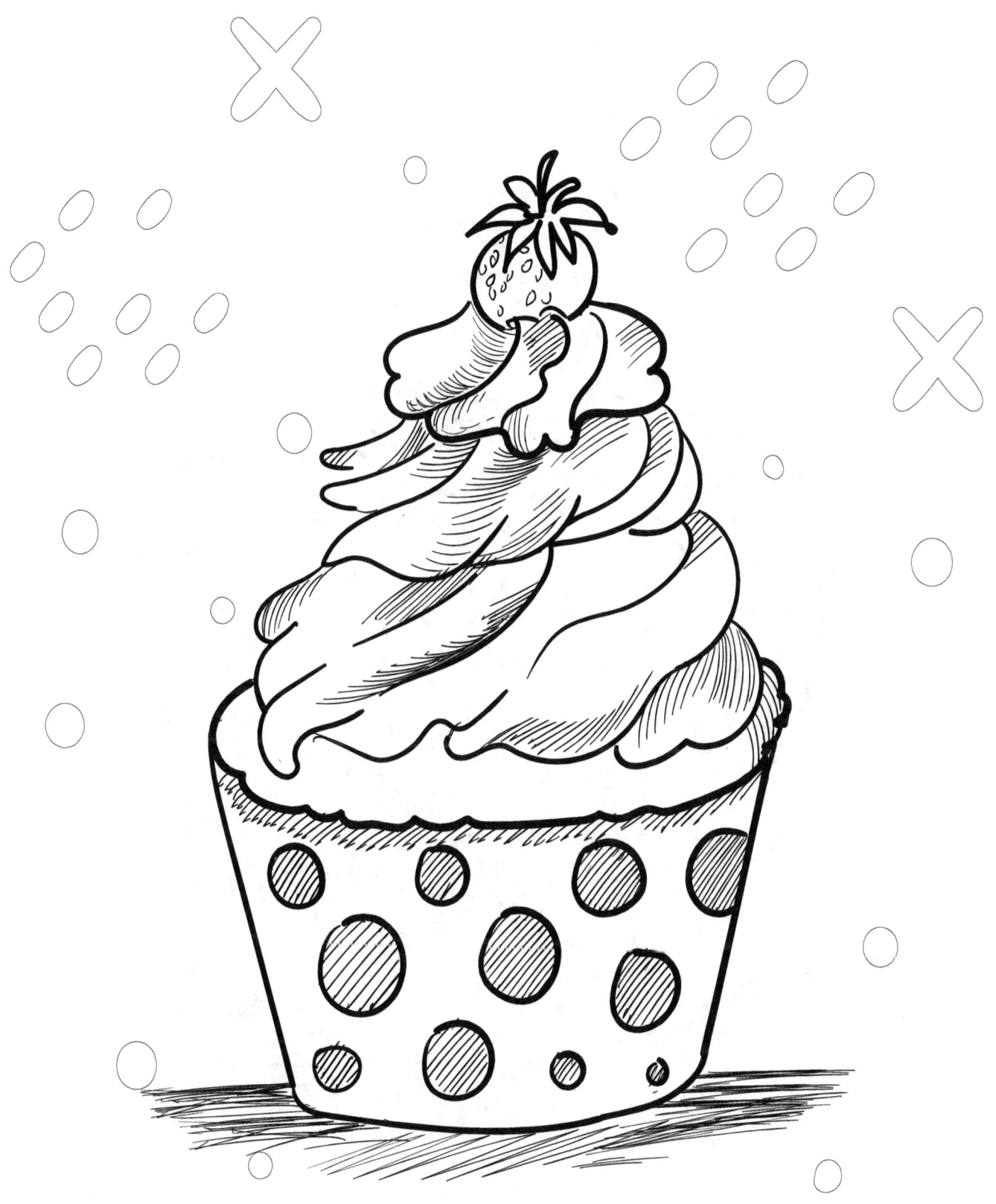

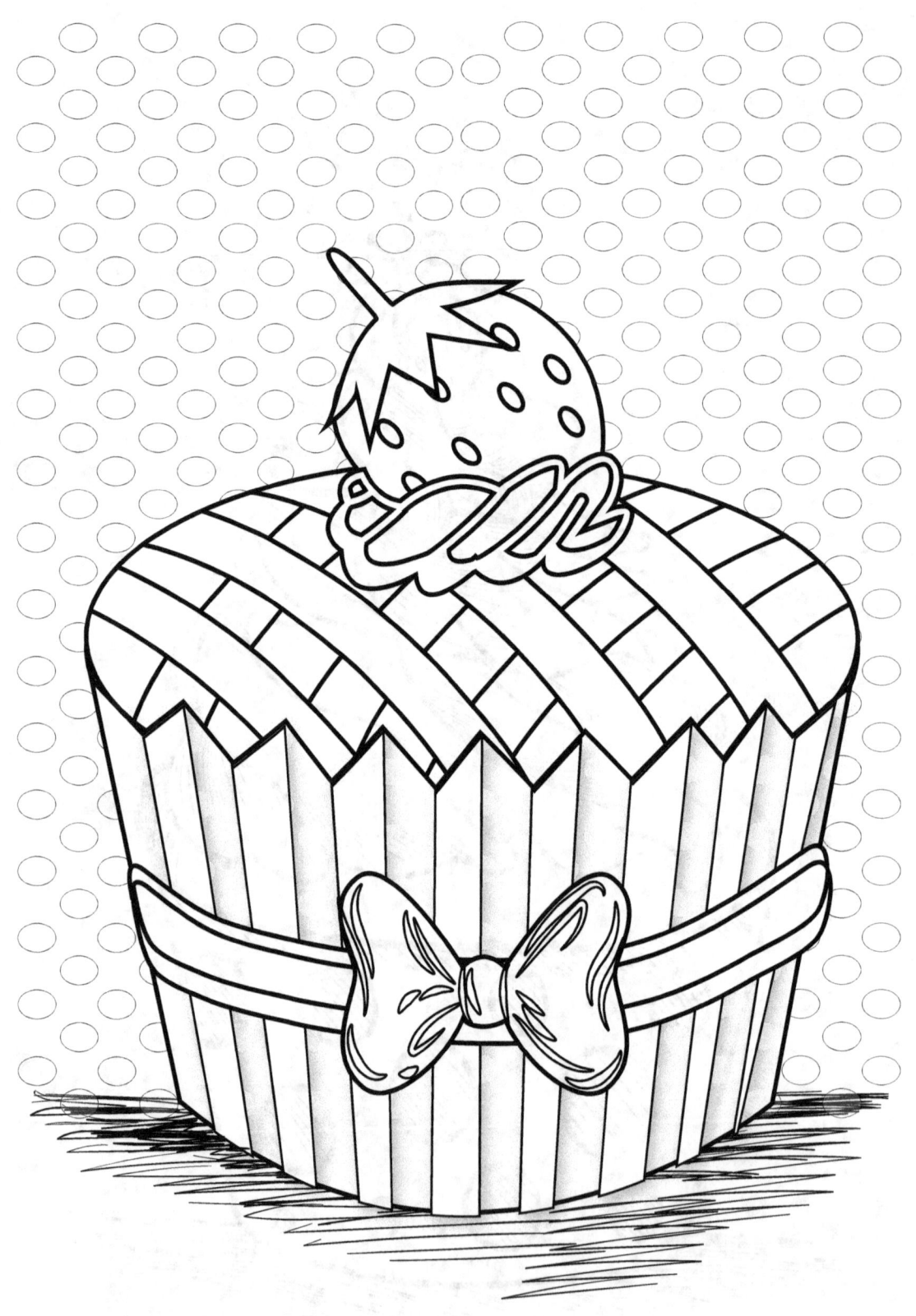

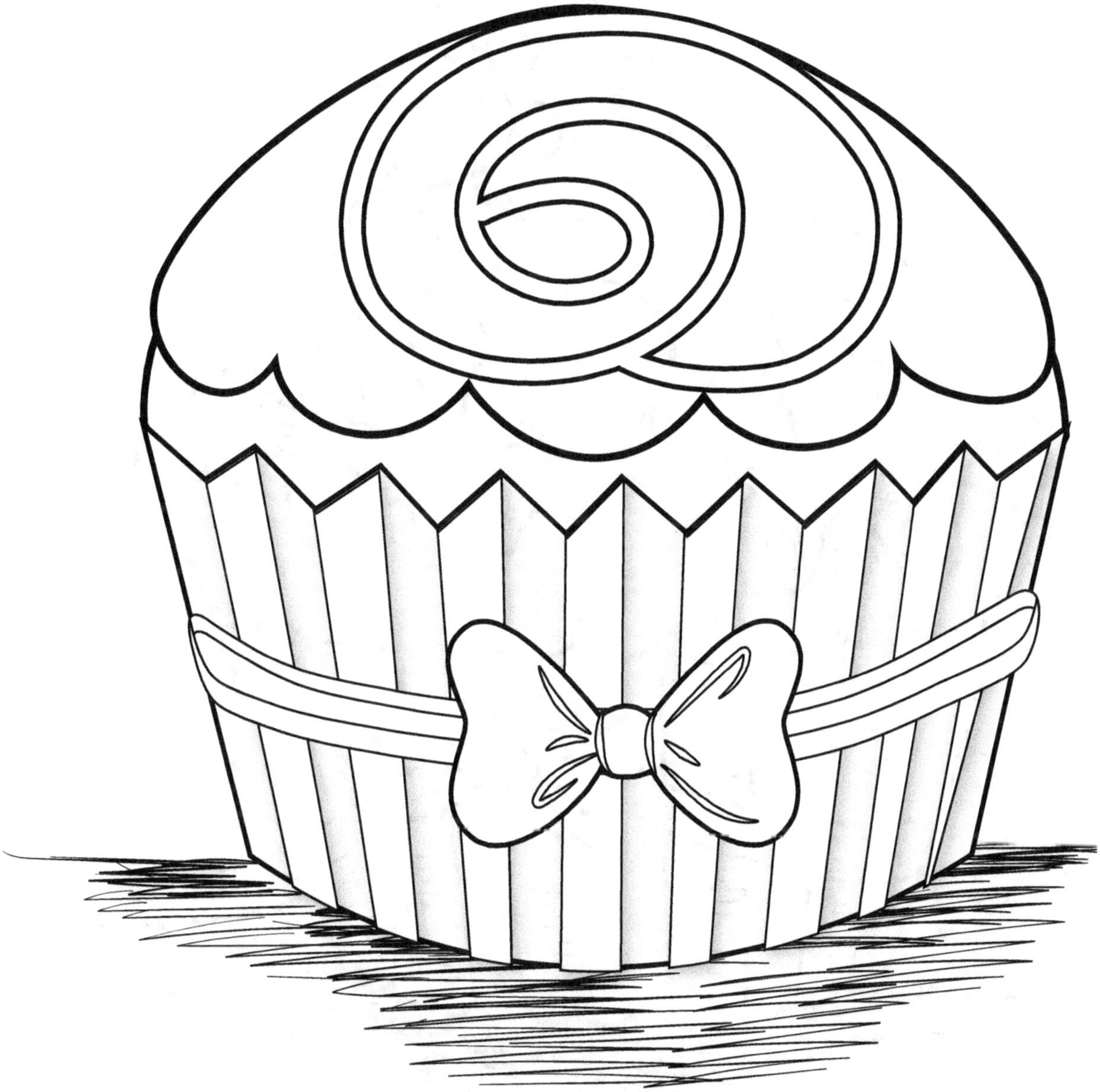

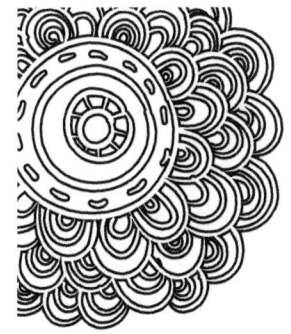
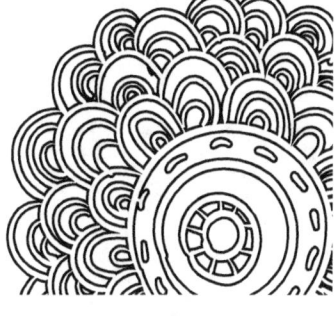

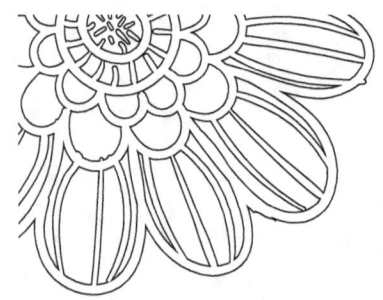

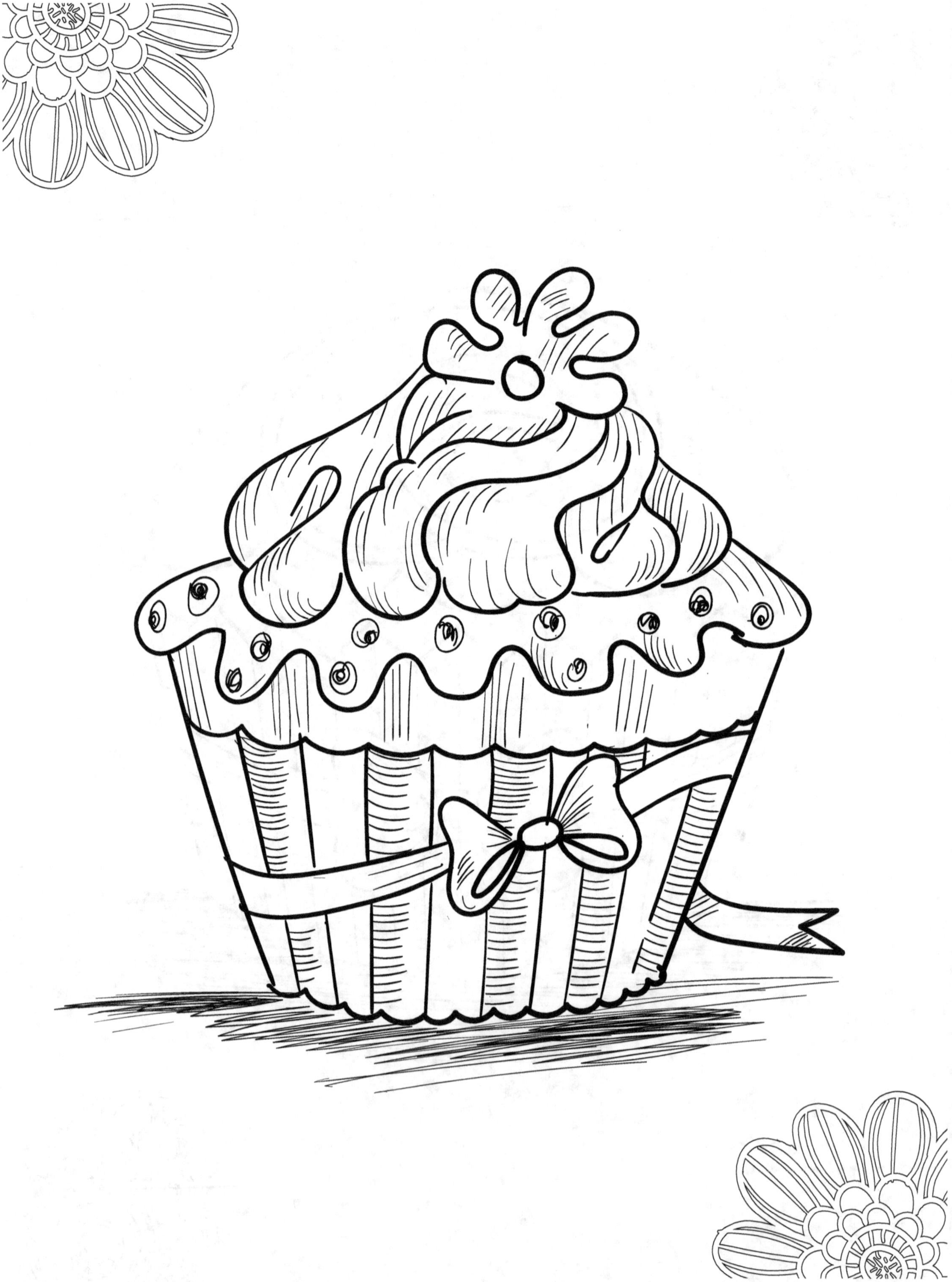

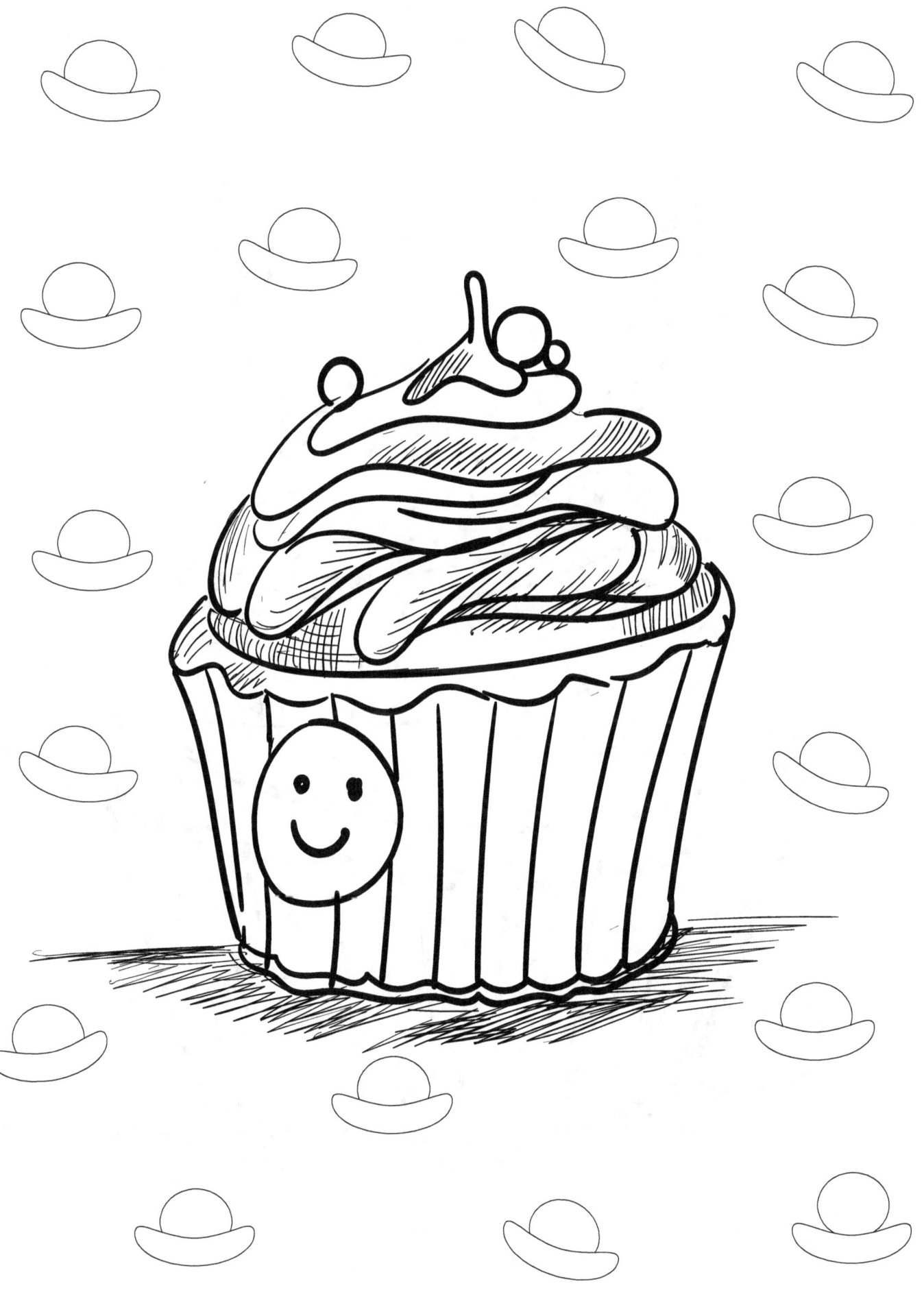

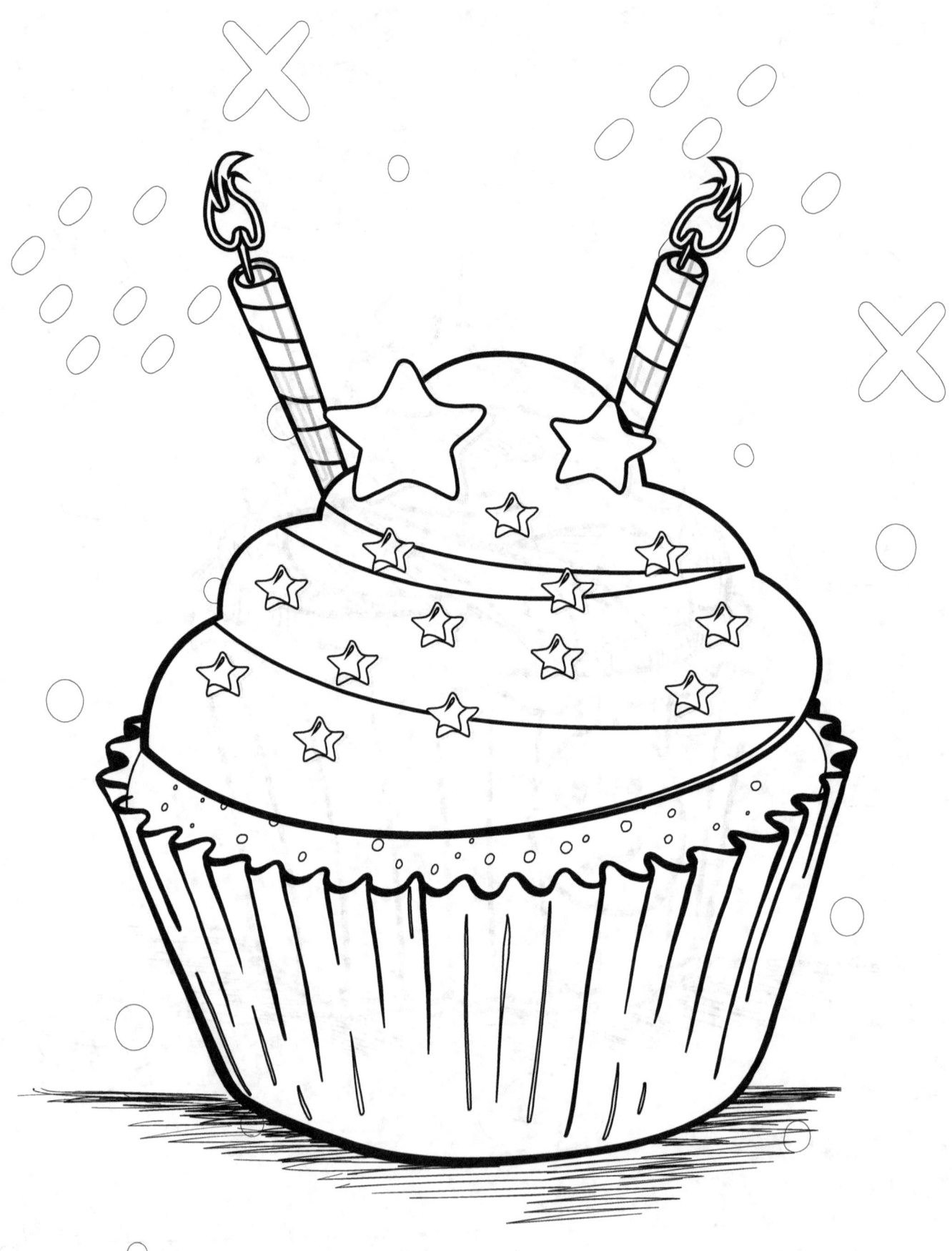

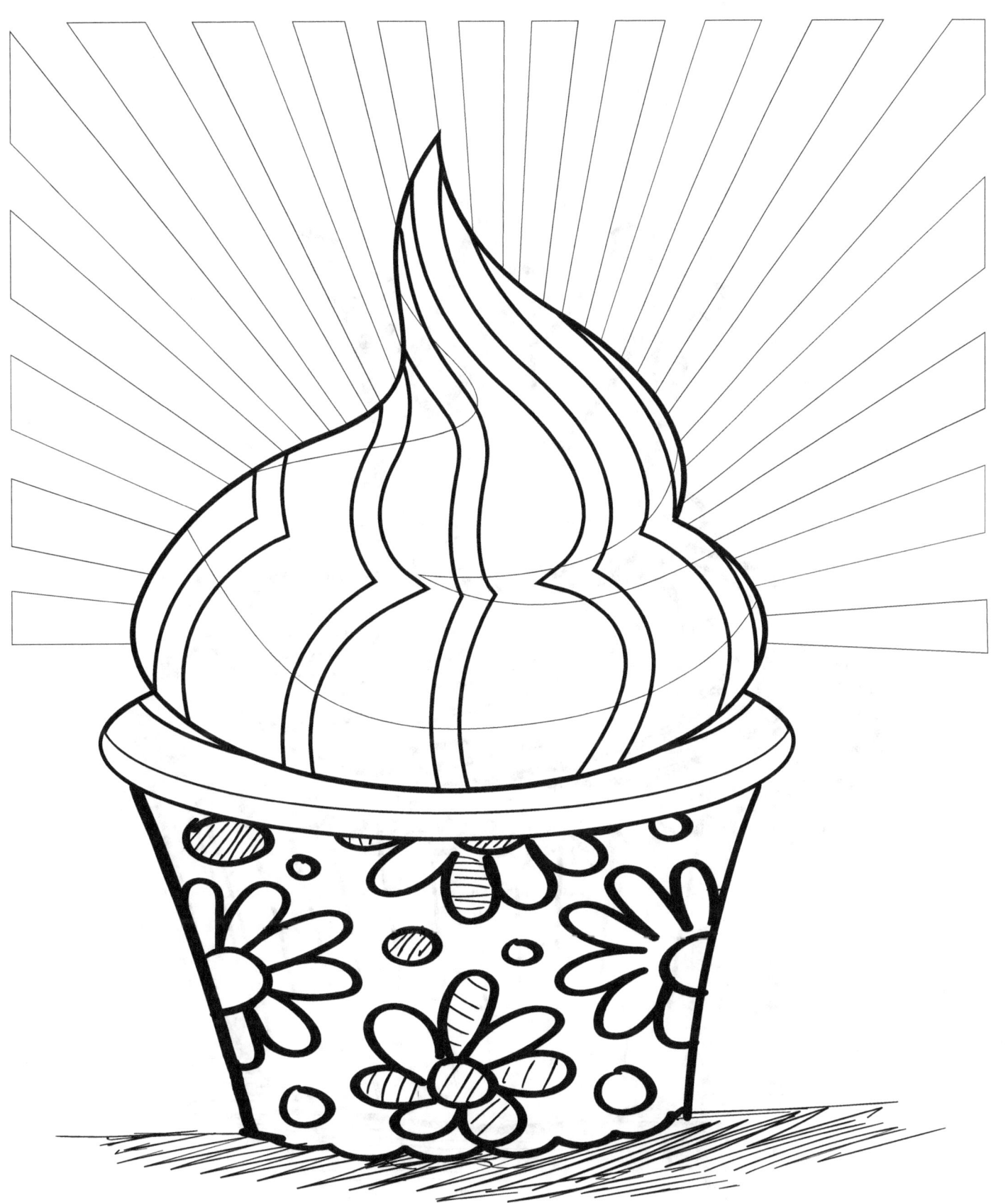

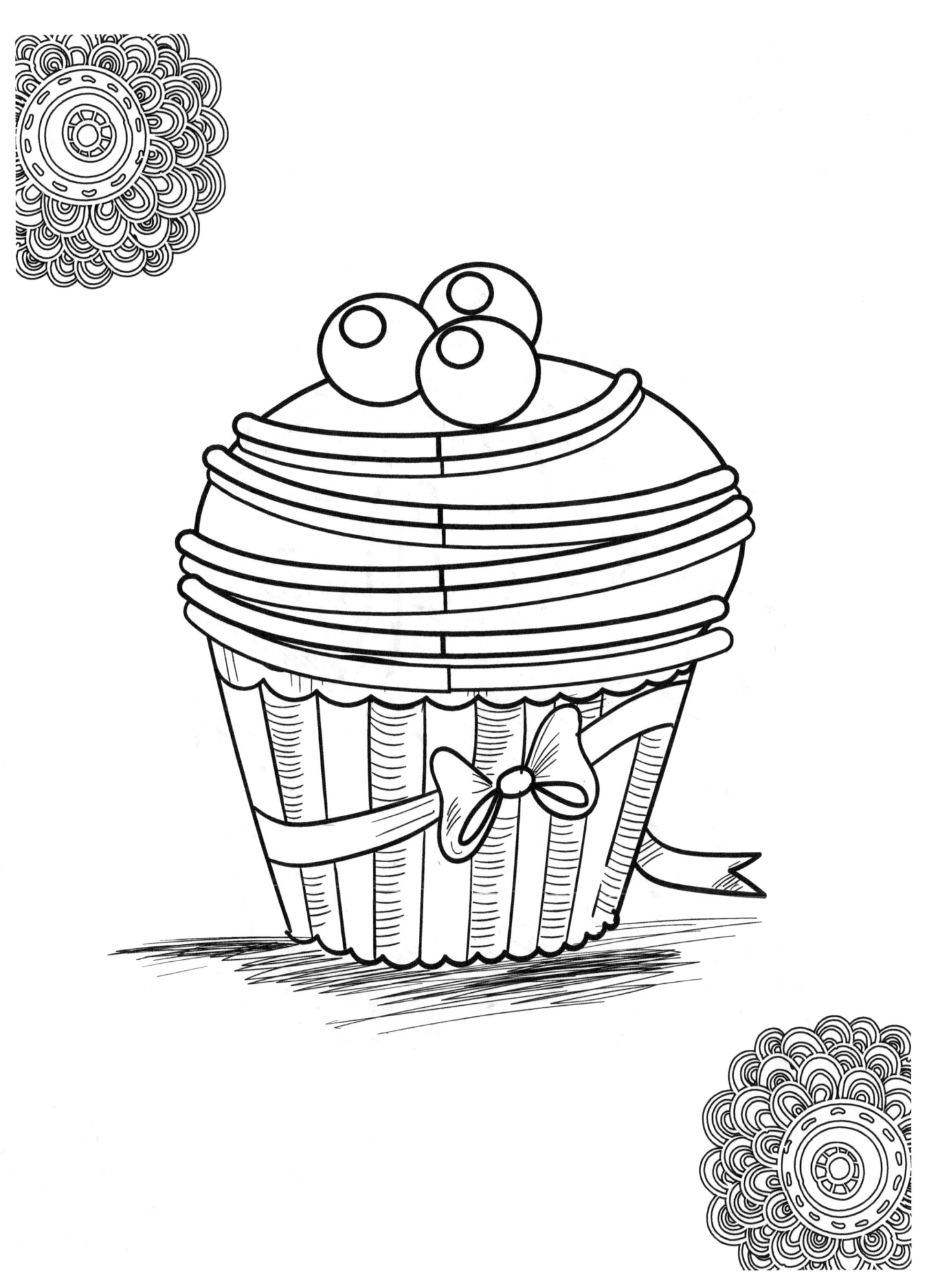

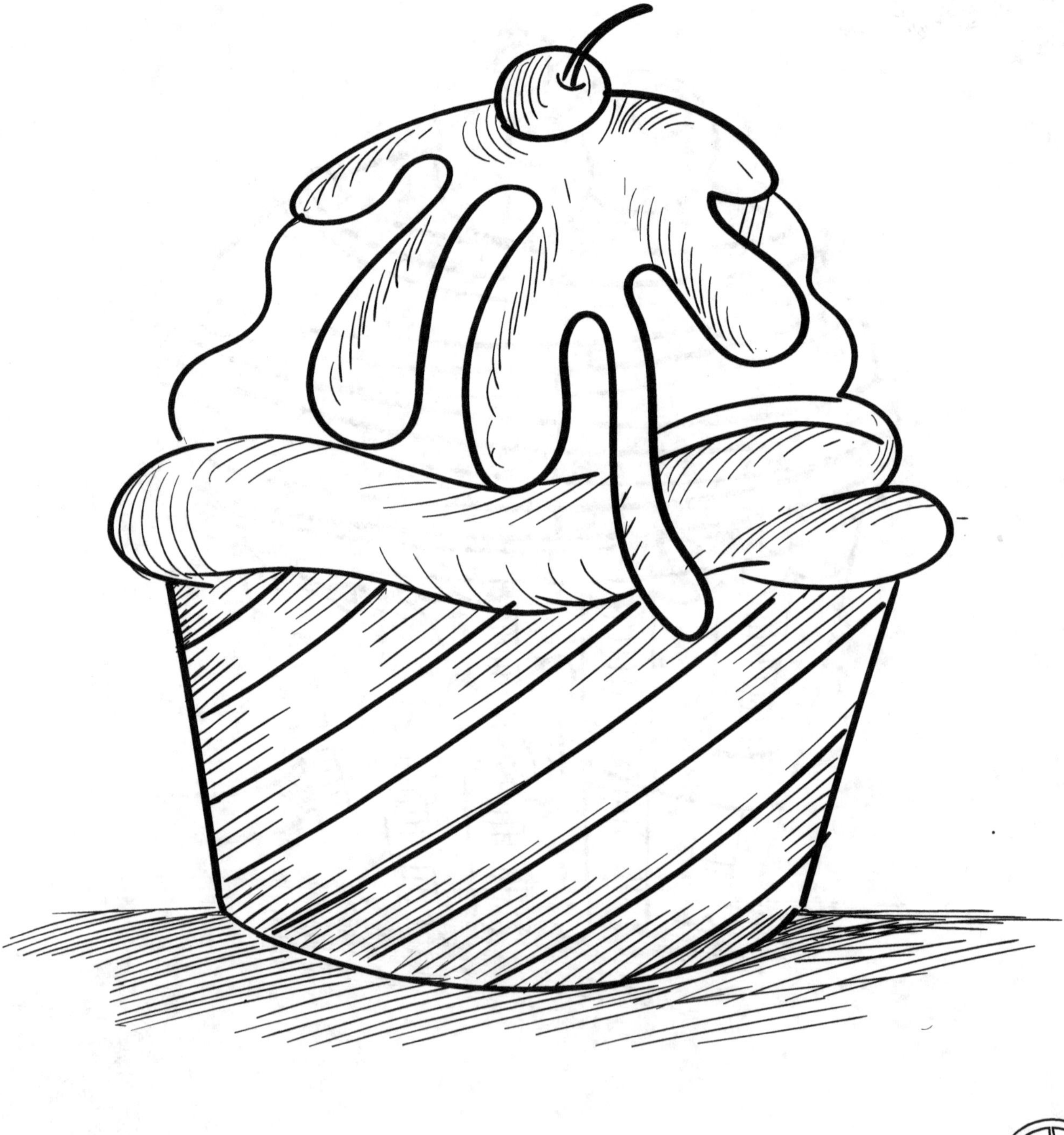

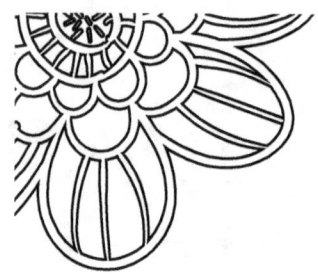

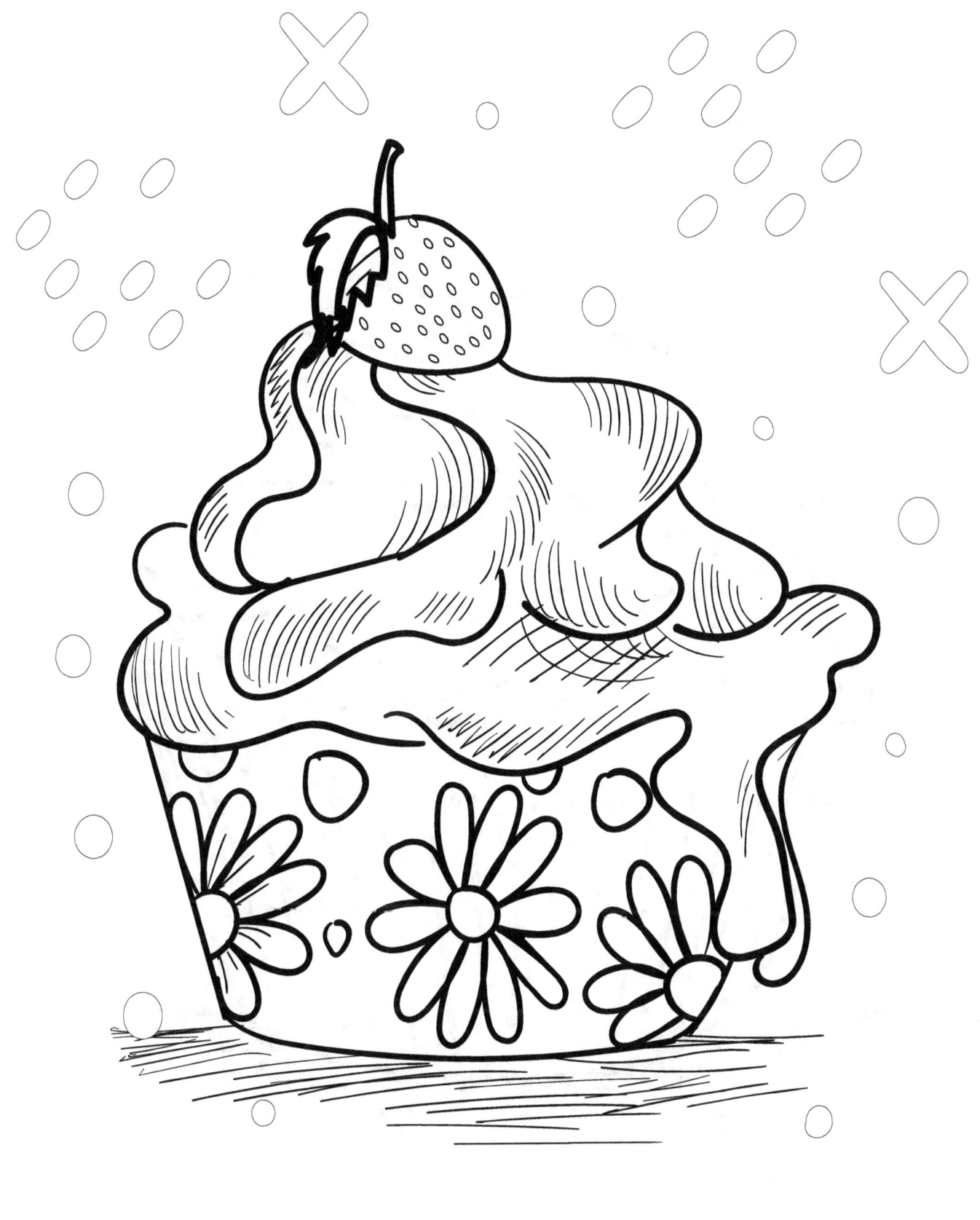

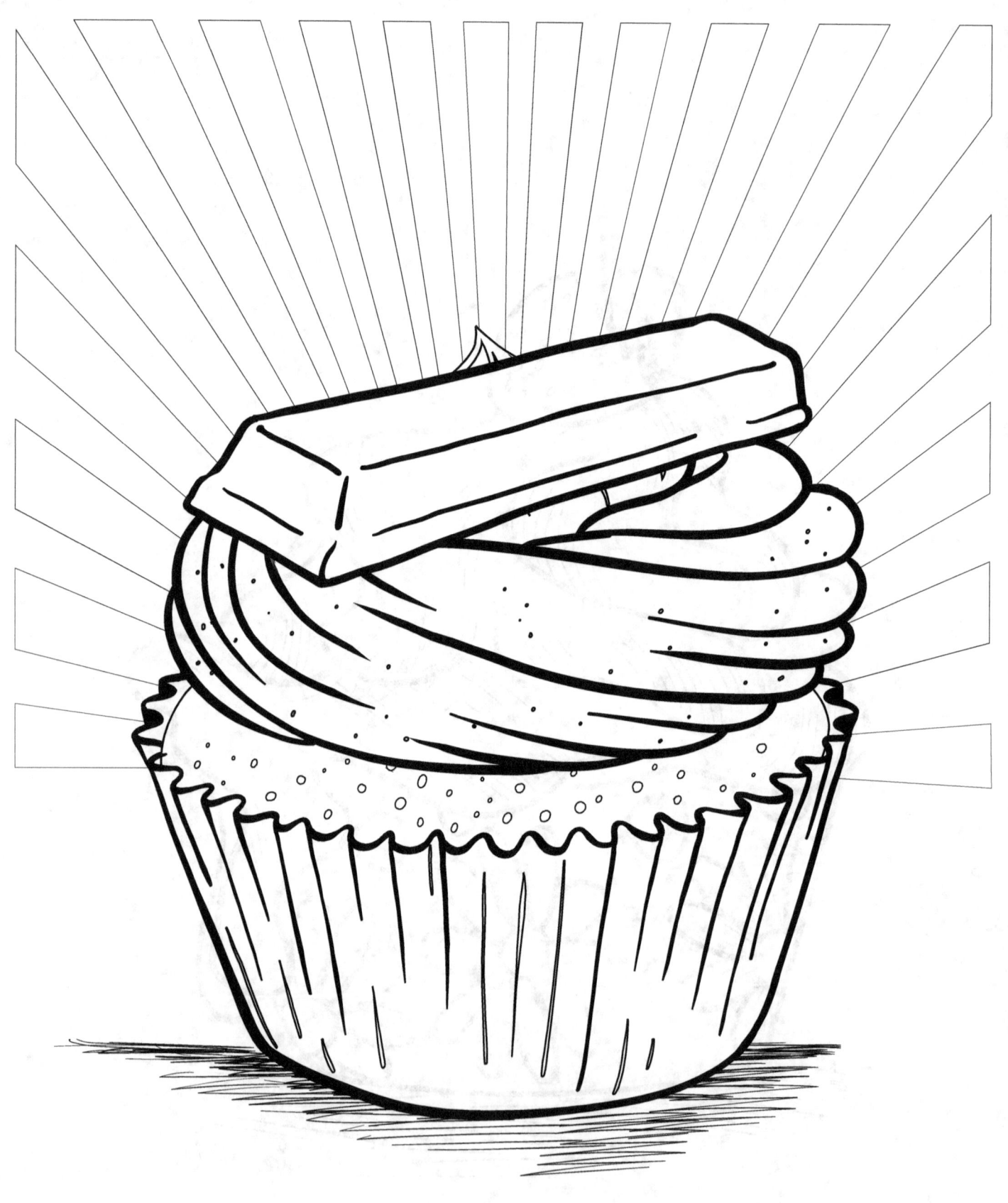

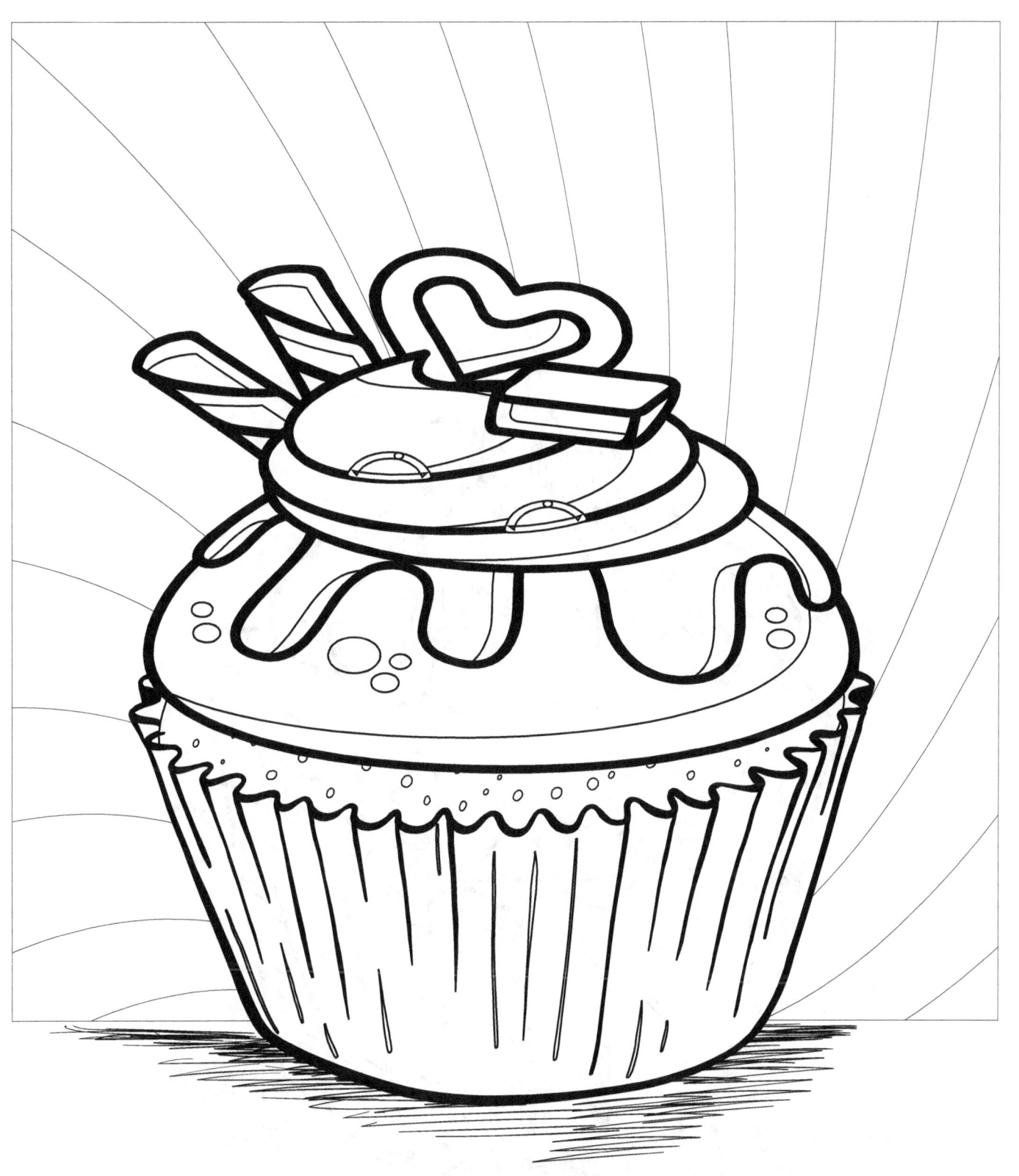

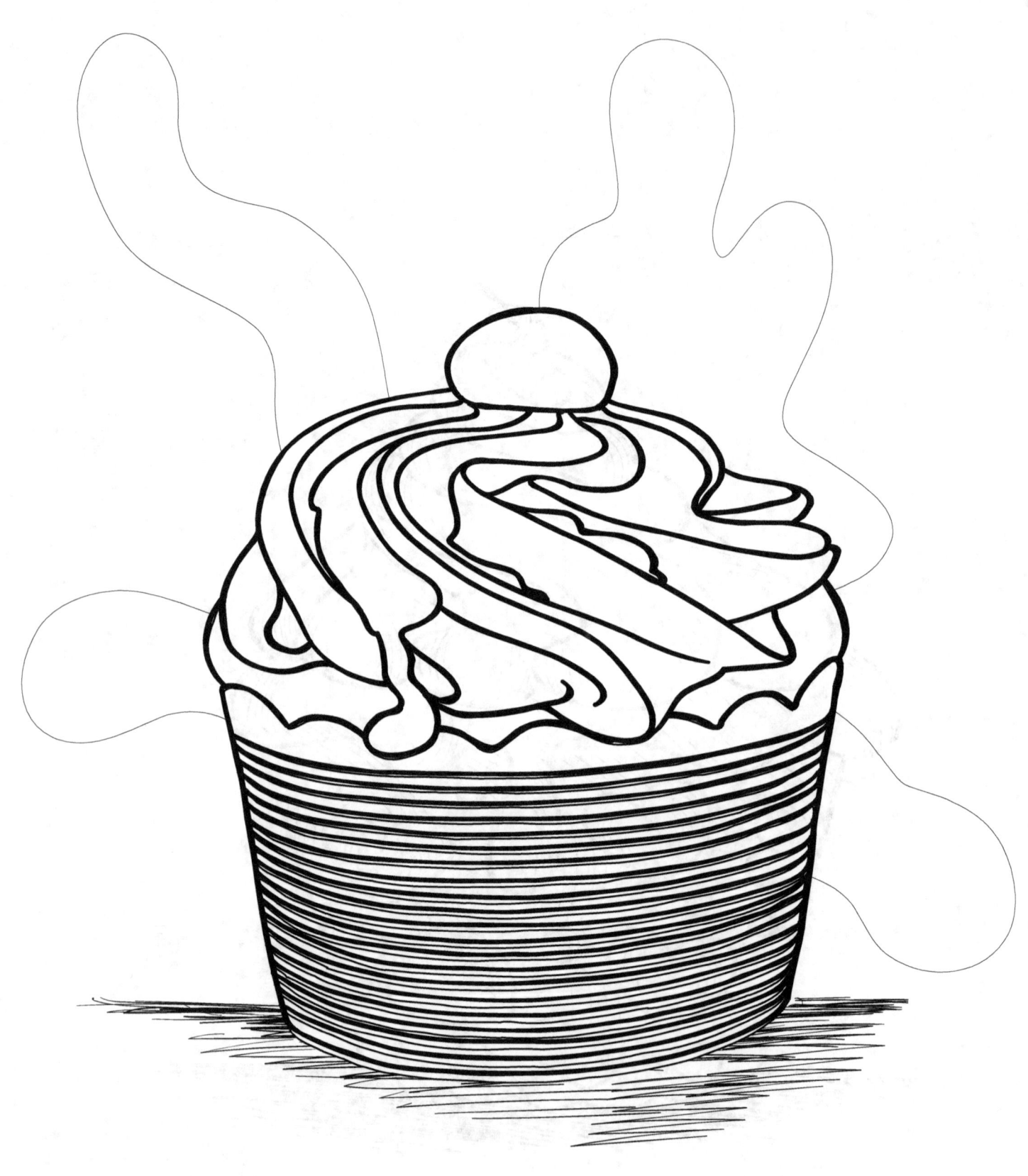

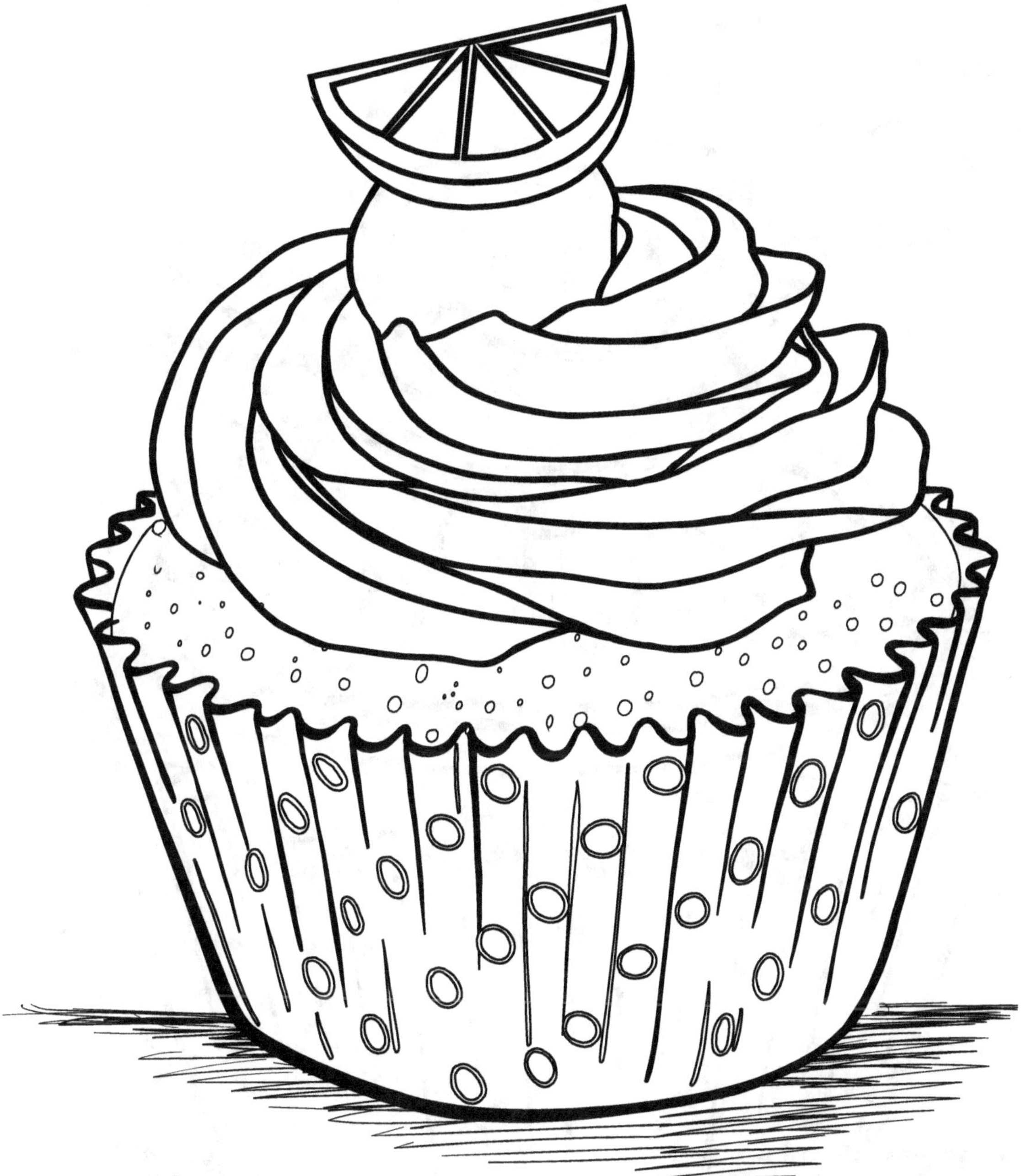

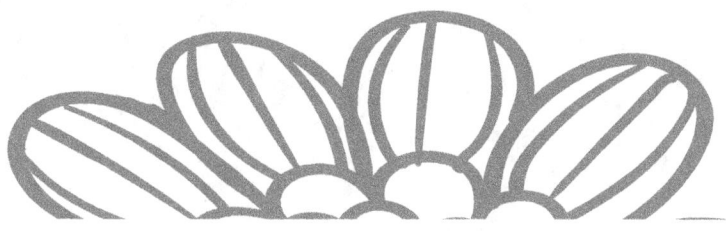

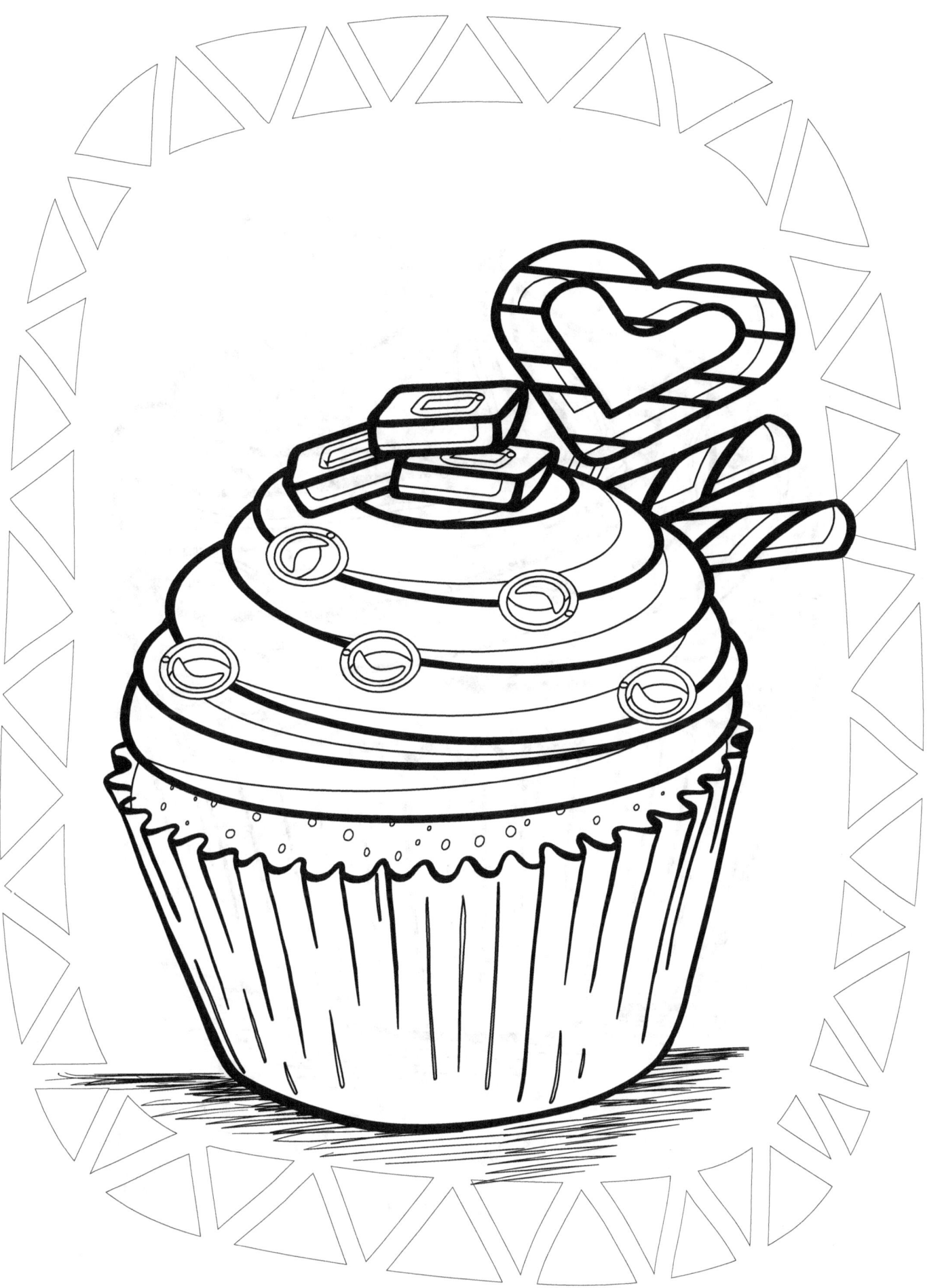

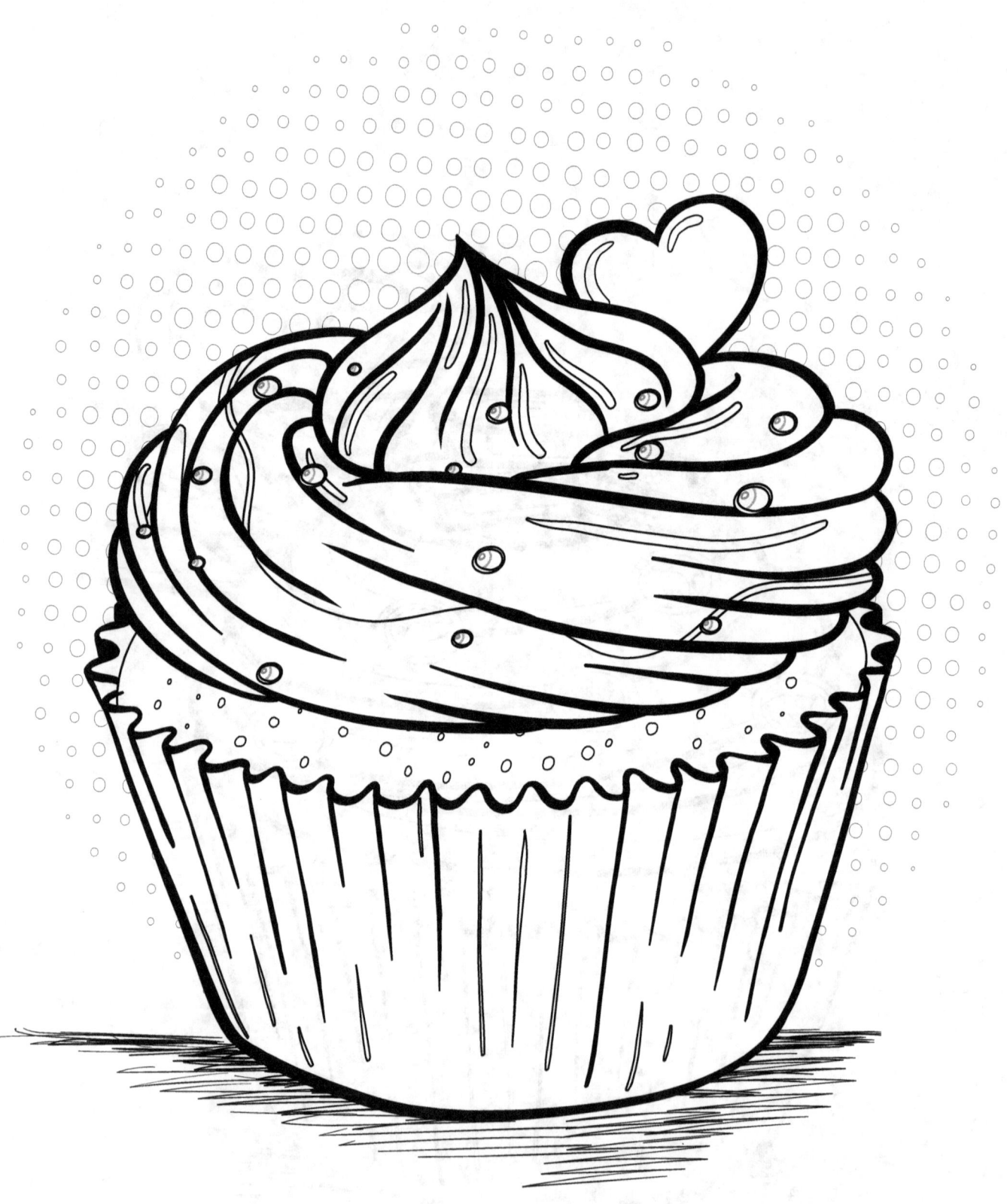

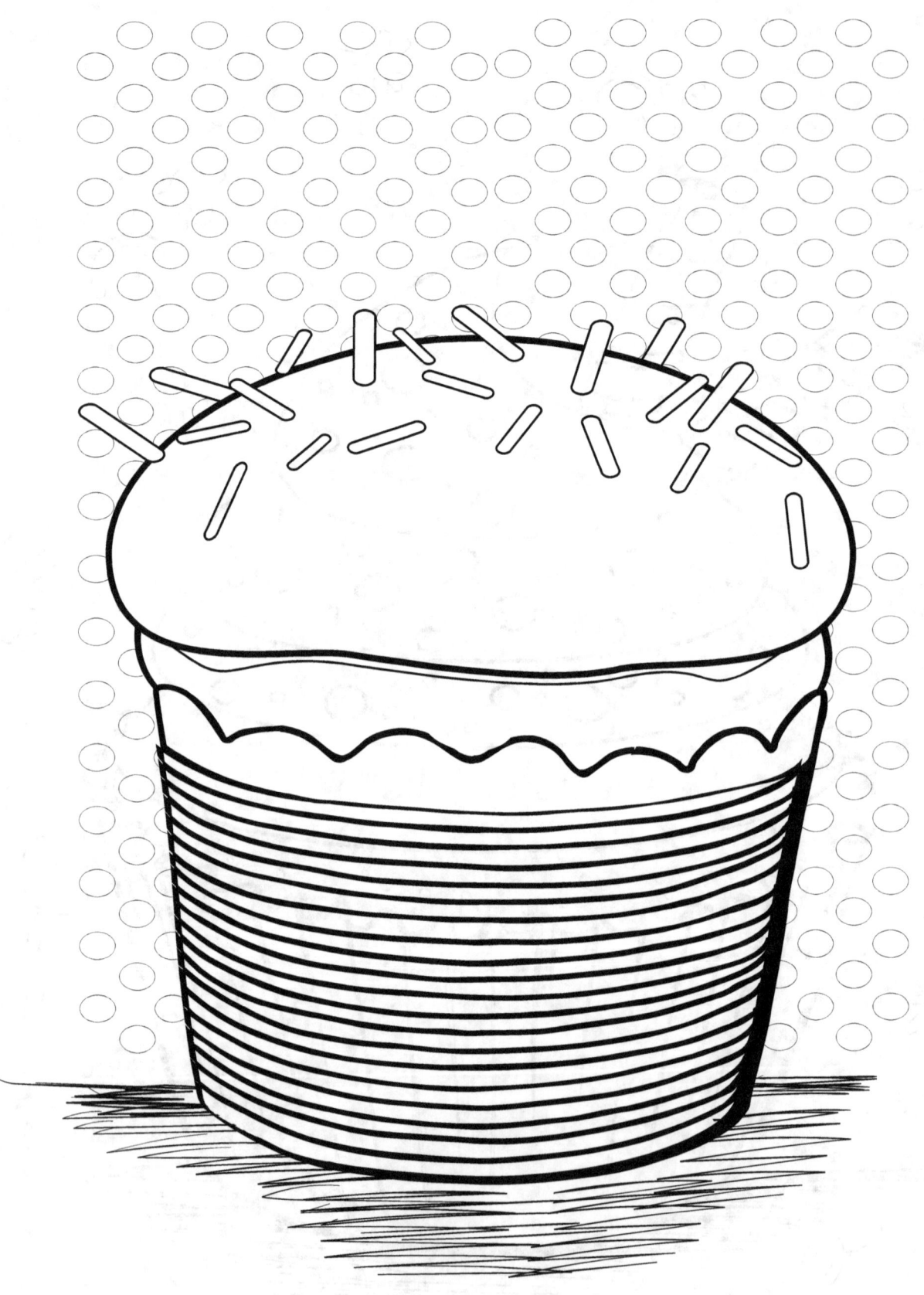

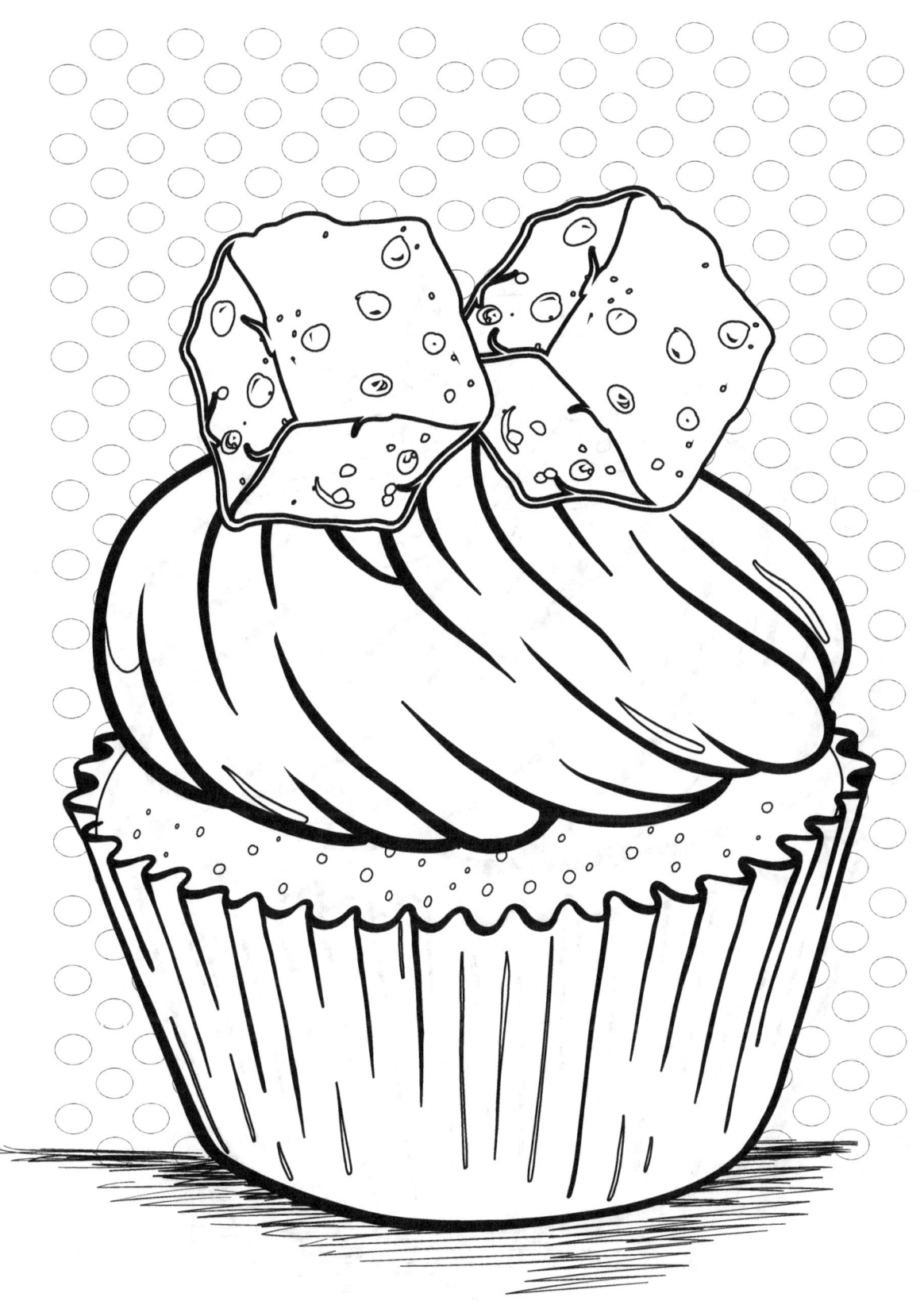

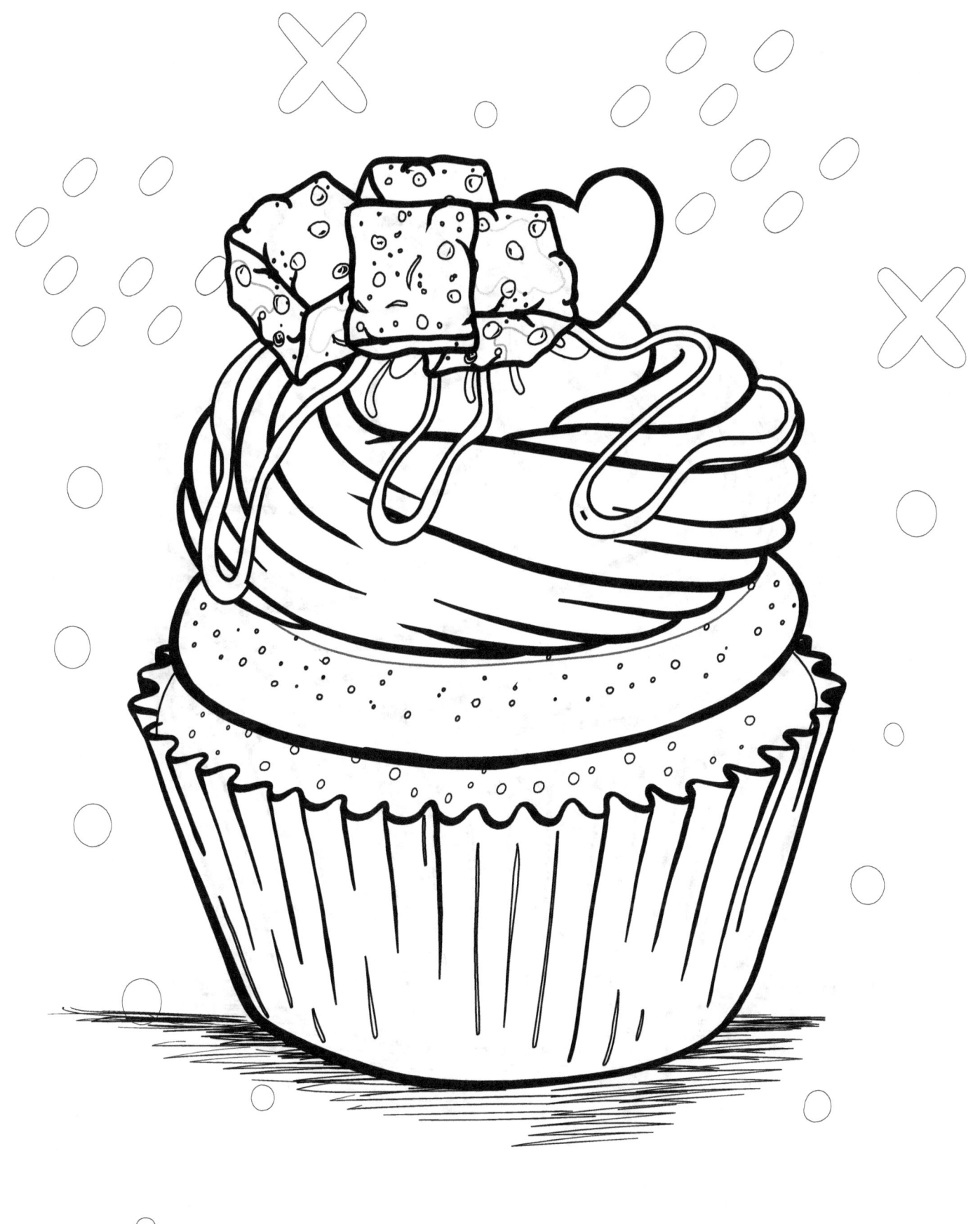

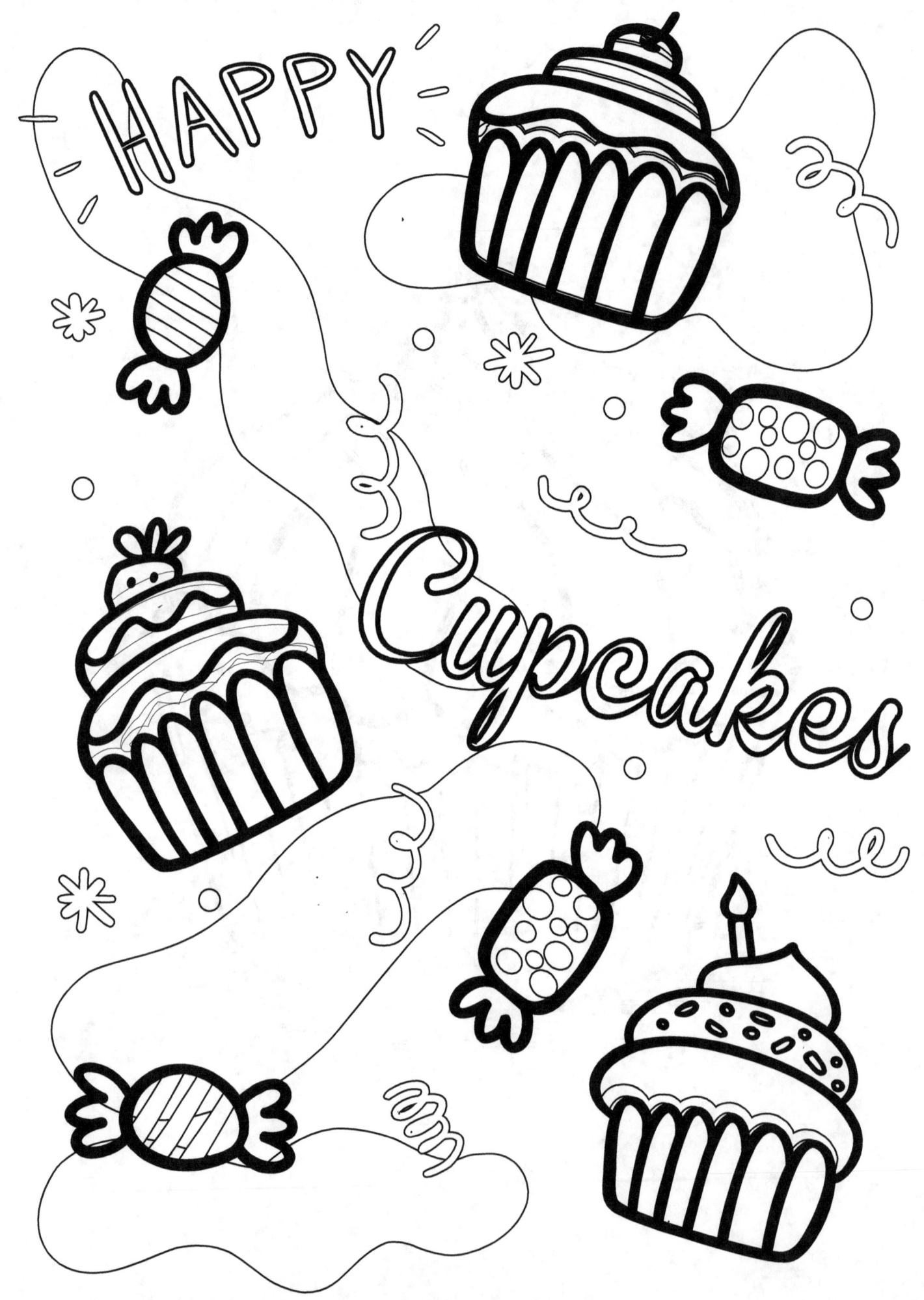

www.ingramcontent.com/pod-product-compliance
Lightning Source LLC
Chambersburg PA
CBHW060440220526
45465CB00008B/3213